UNDERSTANDING
MUSIC
EDUCATION

To Clarie, for everything

In memory of Nancy Stakelum (née Finn) 1930-2020

Sara Miller McCune founded SAGE Publishing in 1965 to support the dissemination of usable knowledge and educate a global community. SAGE publishes more than 1000 journals and over 800 new books each year, spanning a wide range of subject areas. Our growing selection of library products includes archives, data, case studies and video. SAGE remains majority owned by our founder and after her lifetime will become owned by a charitable trust that secures the company's continued independence.

Los Angeles | London | New Delhi | Singapore | Washington DC | Melbourne

UNDERSTANDING MUSIC EDUCATION

Exploring Children's Musical Worlds

MARY STAKELUM

Los Angeles | London | New Delhi
Singapore | Washington DC | Melbourne

Los Angeles | London | New Delhi
Singapore | Washington DC | Melbourne

SAGE Publications Ltd
1 Oliver's Yard
55 City Road
London EC1Y 1SP

SAGE Publications Inc.
2455 Teller Road
Thousand Oaks, California 91320

SAGE Publications India Pvt Ltd
B 1/I 1 Mohan Cooperative Industrial Area
Mathura Road
New Delhi 110 044

SAGE Publications Asia-Pacific Pte Ltd
3 Church Street
#10-04 Samsung Hub
Singapore 049483

Editor: James Clark
Assistant editor: Diana Alves
Production editor: Megha Negi
Copyeditor: Elaine Leek
Proofreader: Camille Bramall
Indexer: Cathryn Pritchard
Marketing manager: Lorna Patkai
Cover design: Naomi Robinson
Typeset by: KnowledgeWorks Global Ltd.,
Chennai, India
Printed in the UK

Library of Congress Control Number: 2021951973

British Library Cataloguing in Publication data

A catalogue record for this book is available from the British Library

ISBN 978-1-4739-1-4346
ISBN 978-1-4739-1-4353 (Pbk)

At SAGE we take sustainability seriously. Most of our products are printed in the UK using responsibly sourced papers and boards. When we print overseas we ensure sustainable papers are used as measured by the PREPS grading system. We undertake an annual audit to monitor our sustainability.

CONTENTS

ABOUT THE AUTHOR

Born in Ireland, **Mary Stakelum** holds degrees from the National University of Ireland (BEd Hons, Carysfort College, Dublin; BMus, University College Cork) and has undertaken postgraduate studies at the Kodály Institute in Kecskemét and at the Institute of Education, University of London, from where she gained her PhD on `Transmission, Transformation and Replication: Case Studies of Practice in an Irish Primary School Setting'. Her publications include journal articles, invited book chapters and edited volumes, and reflect her research focus on aspects of musical development in children and young people, the origin, growth and development of teacher knowledge, and intercultural perspectives on music education. She has been a board member of the European Association for Music in Schools (2013-2017) and, since 2018, a Trustee of the Society for Education and Music Psychology Research (www.sempre.org.uk), serving as their nominated representative on the steering group of Equality, Diversity and Inclusion in Music Studies (edimusicstudies.com). She is editor in chief of *Music Education Research* and director of the biennial international conference on research in music education (RiME). Her teaching experience spans school, conservatoire and university levels. She was appointed Area Leader, Music Education at the Royal College of Music in 2019. Prior to this she has held leadership positions in higher education on a variety of programmes related to music and education (PGCE Secondary Music, BAEd with music specialism, MA Music in Professional Practice, MA Music Education) and doctoral research studies in arts, humanities and social sciences, including education.

ACKNOWLEDGEMENTS

I want to thank my students who have engaged with me in discussions about music education and whose passion and commitment are a constant source of inspiration to me. Special thanks to Dave Camlin, Jess Pitt and Mary Pells, my colleagues on the Music Education team at the Royal College of Music, who remind me of how joyful teaching, learning and research can be. I am indebted to Julia Partington for her generosity and advice on aspects of early childhood education policy. At Sage thanks are due to James Clark for his support of the project and to Diana Alves for encouraging me throughout. I want to record my appreciation of Chartwell Dutiro (1957–2019), who graciously granted me an interview with him in 2015, on aspects of his musical childhood and experiences of music education. I have included material from the interview in the book.

PREFACE

Like many people, I've encountered the full gamut of teachers in my formative experiences and while we might debate about the role played by subject expertise, energy, enthusiasm or some other attribute in defining what makes one teacher more memorable to us than others, we must surely agree that the greatest gift we can get from a teacher is the belief in ourselves that we can achieve our potential. By this I mean not that we can become *the* best but that we can become *our* best and it is this small but not insignificant detail that has led me to present the ideas in this book. I want to explore the concept of music education from the perspective of 'being ourselves' and using this as the starting point, to argue that what the learner offers to the teacher is trust and vulnerability. Framed in this way, education is about being and becoming our best selves in the world.

My concern that the umbrella term 'music education' is increasingly being used as if it has a universally understood meaning has prompted me to begin with a chapter on music education as a field of study. My intention here is to seek out the two concepts – music and education – and explore them separately before putting them back together as a composite. In defining the parameters, I have drawn on Estelle Jorgensen's pictures of music education as I find her way of using metaphor and model very useful in bringing together some complex ideas with a refreshingly lucid absence of jargon. From there it was possible for me to explore ways in which versions of musical childhood have informed the presentation of music in the field of education, with particular reference to its emergence as a school subject in England in recent times.

In Chapter 2 I have tasked myself with setting up two versions of response to the question 'what is?'. The first of these looks at music as an art object and here I have tried to distil the key concepts from philosophical writing on the topic: aware that I can only touch on the vast array of literature that already exists on the topic, I think it is important nonetheless to map out some of the territory for the reader. The second response to the question is to look at music as predicate, as something humans do. In doing this, I am interested in pointing to the origin of such ideas, and for this reason I've included reference to writers whose experience of music as art object has led them to find an alternative. I find this relational aspect compelling.

I am aware that with my approach there's a danger that the two metaphors – the object/artwork/piece and the predicate/working/piecing – will be seen by the reader as an attempt to create binary opposites, which, though not my primary intention, is a risk I'm prepared to take in order to underline a central point underpinning the book: that the concept of 'music as object' has colonised much of the thinking around music education.

In Chapter 3 the focus is on moving from 'what is?' to 'what if?' by exploring the relationship between thinking and doing in music. It draws evidence from research studies which examine children's invented notations, the processes involved in listening to music and ways in which music perception can be defined. I've chosen to explore the concept of imagination rather than creativity, largely because I believe that the latter has enjoyed popularity for some time and there's not enough attention paid in music education to the former. For me, the prospect of considering imagination from the root 'imago' has been helpful in providing an interdisciplinary dimension to a narrative on responses to music: movement, drawing and verbal descriptors are highlighted as ways in which responses to music can be shared or made visible.

Ideas introduced in the earlier chapters are worked out in practice in later chapters. This includes in Chapter 4 attention to the development of musical connoisseurship in the young learner at an early age. Examples are drawn from musical materials devised for pedagogical purposes, methodical approaches to music education of the young, and music selected by adults from versions of musical childhood which range from the solitude and placelessness of the idealised child to those which are socially contextualised and culturally situated.

This theme continues in Chapter 5, though with a shift in emphasis from adult conceptions of musical worlds of children to musical encounters created by children in settings of their own making. The practice of undertaking researching *with* children rather than *on* them, though relatively new, reveals that in playful music making, boundaries between in school and out of school are more fluid than we might expect. We find evidence of this in studies involving children interacting with each other outside school where ways of behaviour mirror those found in the teacher–learner roles in school. Chapter 6 presents four projects which were initiated for children by adults for specific purposes. I've chosen them because, while each one sets out to nurture in the participants a sense of being and/or belonging in the world, the way in which they 'place' or 'situate' the children in the world differs. This raises for me an interesting point about the concept of place and points to the possibility of finding ways in which a conceptualisation of music education can take into account not only the content but the people and the places in which music education occurs. This is a theme to which I return in Chapter 7 as I attempt to bring together the many ideas introduced in the book. In doing this, I've found Gert Biesta's (2022) exploration of world-centred education very helpful. Not only does his interest in looking at education educationally resonate with Estelle Jorgensen's (2011) case for engaging with music education music educationally, but Biesta's ideas also bring to mind the projects which facilitate the discovery by young children of themselves being in the world. For me, the permeation of this awareness of 'who I am' and 'where I am' throughout music education offers the best of all worlds to teacher and learner.

By way of underlining my purpose in writing this book, I conclude this introduction by offering a vignette from my professional practice in the field of initial teacher education. It's accompanied by a reflective task which I hope brings the relevance of the following pages into focus, and sets the reader up for the reflective tasks which are a feature of each chapter.

'Teacher! We're *in* a cuboid!'

When working in teacher education I observed a lesson on maths in a primary school with children aged 8/9. The topic was shapes and the focus was on cuboids. Having done the initial part of the lesson describing the properties of a cuboid, the student teacher asked the young learners to look around the room for examples of cuboids and to raise their hand when they had found some. The children responded with examples such as the tiles on the classroom floor, the wooden panels in the wall, panes of glass in the window, the surface of their desks and so on. As this was happening, I caught sight of one girl waiting patiently for the teacher to ask her, and her hand waving became increasingly more energetic until finally the teacher noticed her and invited her to respond, whereupon she exclaimed with undiluted excitement 'Teacher! We're *in* a cuboid!'. Because of the context – it was an observation of the student teacher's capacity to satisfy the requirements of a lesson format derived from set aims and objectives and the possibility of deviating from a prepared script would have been likely to introduce an element of risk – the teacher's response was to acknowledge the child's response without reference to the delight of the learner's discovery of being in the cuboid. As the teacher moved on to another child, I found myself having to control my own excitement at what appeared to me to be a profound moment of revelation for this young learner – an aha moment or a Eureka moment – and to be reminded of what it feels like to experience these moments of discovery of our place in the world.

How might this relate to your formative experiences, your experience of the musical world and your place within it?

1

AN INTRODUCTION TO MUSIC EDUCATION AS A FIELD OF STUDY

This chapter focuses on:

- Introducing music education as a field of study
- Conceptualising musical childhood in the education system
- Using models and metaphors to depict music education
- Identifying issues concerning the selection of musical content in curriculum

Introduction

This chapter begins by pointing to the many ways in which music intersects with our everyday lives. We look at how our encounters with music in school shape our relationship with ourselves and others from an early age, and can leave a legacy with us that lasts a lifetime. We see this played out in the educational system where some teachers working with young children conclude that music is not something that belongs to them, or is not for them. In trying to understand how this has come to be, we explore the notion of musical childhood as a construct, and how music as a subject in school has been constructed in modern-day England. In doing this, we identify some of the assumptions underpinning music literacy and the creativity movement as two competing discourses. From there we take a broader perspective and draw on the subject of music, teaching, learning, instruction, curriculum and administration to convey pictures of music education using Jorgensen's models and metaphors. The chapter concludes by flagging up issues concerning the selection of musical content in curriculum.

Forming a relationship with music in education

Many of us would accept that music holds a unique place in our lives. We might claim that it connects us with an array of feelings and emotions which are deeply seated within us. We might recognise its potential for enhancing the solemnity of ceremonies and forging meaningful relationships with others. We might associate it with gleeful sounds in the playground, exuberant chants on the football terraces, singsongs at parties and other social events. Whatever our experiences are, it is likely that they have been influenced and shaped by education and yet it is probably true to say that we are seldom called upon to define for ourselves or others how music and education interact with, and relate to, each other. We tend to think that it just happens. This may not be problematic where our experience of the relationship between music and education is positive and life affirming. Music education can inspire us to engage in playful and imaginative musical dialogues with those around us, and to develop our curiosity and fascination with creating new musical worlds. Indeed such is the ready availability of the pleasure and benefits to us we may see no grounds for offering to challenge or critique the status quo.

There are others for whom the relationship between music and education has been less than positive and memories of childhood interactions with music education continue to haunt them through adulthood. They can recall vividly experiences of humiliation, fear and boredom when learning music in school, and they rejected what was on offer at the earliest opportunity.

The identification of these two groups is not accidental and is the starting point for the book. In contending that there are far too many reports of negative formative experiences from teachers of young children I want to highlight the need to move away from the presentation of the professional practice of the classroom teacher as somewhat deficient. This been confirmed to me over and over again both from my own research and practice in music education. The aim is to bring into view some of the invisible threads holding together contemporary conceptions of musical child-hoods, asking how and why they are resistant to change, arguing that they continue to be perpetuated more by myth and folklore than by evidence from those involved in education from the earliest stages. It culminates in a display from this important group in the music education sector of a reticence and resistance to exploring musical worlds in themselves and in the children they encounter. As found in Stakelum and Baker (2013), teachers themselves reported valuing the formative experiences that were for-mal (instrumental lessons for classical music performance) more than those that were not (community singing). Teachers with formal instrumental lessons in their back-ground, that is, those who had been through the training themselves, had the view that music was teachable, while those who had not had lessons, and consequently had no experience of the impact of lessons on their development as 'musicians', reported that music was not teachable. One of our recommendations was to move away from using the label of generalist–specialist to distinguish categories of music educators in the pri-mary school setting. 'If we take the term "generalist teacher" to be the norm for those, who in the course of their professional practice, teach music to pupils in the class-room context, it would seem more appropriate to apply the descriptor "non-generalist" to those who differ from that norm' (p. 151). Furthermore, we found the distinction between 'musician' and 'non-musician' troubling when applied in the musical world of the primary school context. We thought it suggested a deficit state of competence for primary teachers.

At around the same time as this, a review of provision of music education in England (Department for Education, 2011a) led to a government response (Department for Edu-cation, 2011b), culminating in the National Plan for Music Education (Department for Education, 2011c), which set out the parameters for a way ahead for music education. A central part of this was the devising of music education hubs, each one working with clusters of schools 'to determine what high quality music education looks like in a local context, and who will be responsible for the delivery of each aspect' (2011c, p. 16).

Interestingly, in the intervening decade or so, some of the issues remain, namely around the perceived inequity of provision, and the dominance of western classical music in discourse and dialogue. Debates on music in education continue to be fractured and fractious; preconceived ideas about music education remain unchallenged; and learning to play a musical instrument continues to be promoted as the pathway to 'good' music (see Department for Education, 2021a; 2021b).

Pictures of music education

Estelle Jorgensen recognises the importance of the practice of music education and argues that foundational disciplines such as philosophy, psychology and sociology have a role to play in understanding how music education can be conceptualised. Yet they are supplemental to examining music education educationally; that is, in thinking of music education in ways that are grounded in the nature and work of music education itself. She proposes a set of pictures which exemplify ways in which to capture this, and draws on two structural devices to compile them. These are the model and the metaphor. As a concept, the model will be familiar to those involved in education. At policy level, model curricula are presented for implementation by teachers in schools (for a recent example in music education, see Department for Education, 2021b). Teachers use models to present complex ideas in terms that can be readily grasped by the learner. Learners use models to create replicas of what they have been taught in order to evidence their understanding. Jorgensen argues that teachers draw on metaphor in their practice too: 'much of our talk about how to play and sing and the various characteristics of music is metaphoric' (2011, p. 2). This extends to the musical terms used in practice, with musicians referring to the sonic elements such as 'bright' and 'dark' tones, 'thick' and 'thin' textures, and so forth. Because much of the way in which music is experienced and discussed is metaphoric – both literally in terms of sonic elements or particular practices associated with these sounds, and figuratively in terms of what these sounds stand for – Jorgensen suggests that it seems reasonable to view music education metaphorically.

She puts together a series of pictures of music education, each one conceptually distinct, yet with six elements which are common to all:

- the field of study or practice, in this case, music;
- teaching or the means and ends whereby the one-knowing passes on knowledge or wisdom to the one-who-does-not-yet-know;
- learning, the means and ends whereby one comes to know and transform the subject matter (music) and other things;
- instruction, the means and ends of interactive engagement of teacher and student in a pedagogical setting;
- curriculum, the means and ends whereby learners engage with the subject matter (music); and
- administration, or the means and ends of organising the context in which instruction transpires. (p. 12)

The models

Jorgensen explores the notion of the model as it applies to music education and identifies 12 – consumption, apprenticeship, production, rule, pedagogy, community, transgression, growth, healing, energy, informality and connectivity – which she arranges into two groups each with similar aims and methods in respect of the six elements (see Table 1.1).

Table 1.1   Jorgensen's models of music education

Group 1	Group 2
Consumption	Community
Apprenticeship	Transgression
Production	Growth
Rule	Healing
Pedagogy	Energy
	Informality
	Connectivity

The models can be grouped according to differences in approach to each of the six characteristics. For instance, the first group fosters traditional views of music that are conservative in their emphasis on the past, while the second emphasises new music in ways that challenge musical traditions.

Regarding approaches to teaching, one group takes a didactic approach whereas another is more conversational. The first emphasises receptive learning, the second constructivist learning. The first features a hierarchical interaction between teacher and students, while the second is egalitarian. The first features pre-set, subject-centred, product-oriented and convergent curricular, and the second rhapsodic, serendipitous, divergent, people-centred and process-oriented curricula. The first is administered tightly and formally, while the second is administered loosely and informally (2011, p. 260).

The model of apprenticeship, for example, has been used to describe ways of transmitting and transforming musical traditions, cultivating musical skills, and ensuring a continuing supply of skilled professional musicians in particular musical practices. Jorgensen outlines what music education institutions subscribing to this model of music education might encourage in order to achieve their aim:

> musical training, whereby teachers teach by precept and example; formal and informal means of musical learning; the exercise of choice, allowing students and teachers to select their teachers and students, respectively; individual and group instruction tailored to student abilities, summative evaluations to ensure that professional standards are attained and maintained; and institutions such as conservatoires established to ensure formal instruction and the provision of resources needed to accomplish this task. (p. 255)

There are some parallels between the model of apprenticeship and others. Take for example the model of production described by Jorgensen as follows:

> with its focus on teaching musical skills and employing standardised teaching methods that impress knowledge into studies, emphasising learning approaches that are efficient, standardised and scientific, and that prompt receptive learning; operating instruction in a hierarchical fashion in which a one-way, formal, rational, and didactic transmission of information to students prevails; regarding and treating curriculum as a standardised and rationalised system in which predictable outcomes can be expected; making sure of

summative evaluation as a means of assessing outcomes and efficiency in the process; and operating efficiency-driven and data-driven management systems to organise music education. (p. 256)

While both the model of apprenticeship and the model of production share some aspects – the emphasis on training in musical skills, and instruction as a means of operating – they differ in other respects. There is less emphasis on freedom to choose teacher and learner, for example, in the production model and this is certainly true of the context within which learning takes place in the formal institutional school setting.

By contrast, the growth model presents a set of aims which allow more freedom than either apprenticeship or production. The aim of this model is 'to benefit people through facilitating the natural development of their musical self-expression and musical aptitude and potential, and through accomplishing these aims, enrich culture' (p. 256). Like production and apprenticeship, growth seeks to transform musical traditions, but it goes further than this in that it wants also to transform the people who make and take music and develop musical communities through creating rich musical environments and nurturing people individually and collectively. So while all of these share the aim of transformation, only the model of growth extends this to the environment. 'Teaching focuses on cultivating a musical environment in which learning takes place holistically, naturally, and pleasurably in ways appropriate to maturation' (p. 256). Freedom is promoted through the emphasis on aesthetic and artistic value and fostering new and divergent musical expressions. This is not to say that production and apprenticeship deny freedom or apply restrictions which are counter-educational but that freedom is not a defining characteristic of the approach to be found in them. It is at this level of detail that Jorgensen's pictures can be useful in revealing the sometimes subtle differences in emphasis between one approach to aspects of music education and another. It underlines too an important point about assumptions of shared understanding about the aims of music education: 'music education insofar as it is pictured above, draws on a variety of aims, and these aims differ in their salience and potency' (p. 259). It helps to articulate the distinctiveness by looking for some explanatory power. '[S]pecific combinations affect the character of the model, and in cases where the general aims are similar, the specifics of the model play out quite differently in each case' (p. 259). So, while we would expect music education to be concerned with enriching culture and benefiting people, Jorgensen's analysis of practices points out that there are differences in the degree to which these aims are emphasised.

The metaphors

The practice of using metaphors to describe teachers is not unusual and forms part of the lore around education. Metaphors such as teacher as carer or teacher as master will be familiar to us and we would not be surprised to find reference to them in discussions about education. What may not be so apparent to us is the extent to which each of these is underpinned by its own set of values and beliefs about education. When we go beneath the surface of these metaphors, we might expect a carer to prioritise growth and nurturing over training or indoctrination, for example, whereas the focus in the teacher as master might favour discipline and virtuosity over pleasure and self-expression. Jorgensen explores this in relation to music education and identifies 12 metaphors, categorised into two groups – place and role – which can be summarised as follows:

- Place: courtroom, boutique, factory, village, garden, home, seashore, web
- Role: therapist, artist, revolutionary, guide

Each one is underpinned by a set of values. Though the values are held individually, culturally and institutionally, and are promoted and supported in a variety of ways, not all values are held to be of equal weight. Take for example the metaphors of boutique and factory, both of which are places of commerce (see Table 1.2).

Table 1.2 Values identified by Jorgensen (2011) in the metaphors of boutique and factory

Boutique	Factory
Specialisation	Standardisation
Service	Objectification
Efficiency	Commodification
Commodification	Competition
Competition	Predictability
Differentiation	Efficiency
Fashion or sensuous appeal	Functionality
	Mechanisation

Whilst each has its own distinct set of values – the boutique favours differentiation while the factory values standardisation and predictability – both are driven by commodification, competition and efficiency, and this connects them and distinguishes them from the values found in other places appearing on the list.

> Efficiency is the most compelling value because the objective of companies is to make a profit, and if not a profit (in the case of not-for-profit corporations), at least to break even and be accountable and transparent to shareholders in the enterprise. (2011, p. 253)

By contrast, both the home and the garden are places associated with caring, with metaphors rooted in the family being in evidence (see Table 1.3). Values such as love and work are of special importance in each, and play out similarly and differently in each place.

Jorgensen (2011) notes that, of all of the metaphors, the artist and the guide are probably those most commonly associated with a portrayal of the music educator (see Table 1.4). The artist's concern is with aesthetic and artistic values, alongside inspiration, discipline, practices, self-expression, idealisation, canonisation, esotericism, elitism, caring and

Table 1.3 Values identified by Jorgensen (2011) in the metaphors of home and garden

Home	Garden
Particularity	Naturalism
Domesticity	Formality
Informality	Informality
Love	Caring
Idealism	Experience
Spirituality	Growth
Caring	Particularity
Happiness	
Play	
Work	
Fidelity	

virtuosity. For a guide, a different array of values is implicated including pluralism, practicality, pleasure, specialisation, clarity, innovation, communication, serendipity, dialogue and sensation (p. 253). Both are concerned with formation, but the means by which they achieve this differs. Whereas the artist focuses on music making and taking, the guide emphasises the process by which the musician is formed: the artist looks for specific ends, whereas the guide fixes on the path by which to reach the goal.

Table 1.4 Values identified by Jorgensen (2011) in the metaphors of artist and guide

Artist	Guide
Aesthetic	Pluralism
Artistic	Practicality
Inspiration	Pleasure
Discipline	Specialisation
Practice	Clarity
Self-expression	Innovation
Idealisation	Communication
Canonisation	Serendipity
Esotericism	Dialogue
Elitism	Sensation
Caring	
Virtuosity	

Freedom is identified as a value in the metaphor of village and of revolutionary (see. Table 1.5) though the way in which this is understood is likely to be different in each. Freedom to preserve and celebrate a particular set of customs will connect members of the village. For the revolutionary freedom means resisting the status quo, and moving into new worlds and ways of being. In each case, the weight placed on tradition is different, and leads to discussions about which, and whose, decisions to take into account when defining how freedom is to be articulated.

Table 1.5 Values identified by Jorgensen (2011) in the metaphors of village and revolutionary

Village	Revolutionary
Caring	Violence
Exclusivity	Dislocation
Inclusivity	Transformation
Dialogue	Utilitarianism
Equality	Holism
Freedom	Dialogue
Romanticism	Heroism
Nostalgia	Evangelicalism
Tradition	Freedom
Simplicity	Resistance
Identity	Praxis

As with all the metaphors presented, there are questions to be raised about whose values should prevail: '[m]atters of value are interconnected with questions of institutional involvement in music education and the particular roles they do and should play' (p. 254).

By portraying music education in this way, Jorgensen provides us with a lens through which to understand music education and the values underpinning one conception over those underpinning another. She then selects one from each of the sets of metaphor and model to form a picture.

- Boutique and consumption
- Village and community
- Artist and apprenticeship
- Revolutionary and transgression
- Factory and production
- Garden and growth
- Therapist and healing
- Court and rule
- Seashore and energy
- Home and informality
- Guide and pedagogy
- Web and connectivity

Each picture can stand on its own to reveal a particular version of music education. Taken together, they present something about the way in which values are reflected in music educational ideas and practices, offering teachers a means to bring together disparate things, and opening up new ways to understand practice. 'Beyond the grand narratives of the either/or concepts that have too often characterised music educational thinking, they have a modest purpose of opening other fruitful avenues for understanding the ways in which people come to know music' (2011, p. 18).

Jorgensen's list of 12 pictures is by no means exhaustive and she is careful to point out the folly of seeing them as set in stone. They shed light on the complexities around understanding music education as a field of study: clarifying 'why and how disagreements and misunderstandings can emerge when music educators approach the task of mapping the field conceptual at differing levels of generality' (2011, p. 264). She presents them as a way of helping on a practical level and to underline the fact that what we do as music educators is connected to what we think. We do not act in a vacuum and part of the responsibility is to recognise this, and to understand that our actions and practices will change over time, as will the contexts within which our practice takes place. '[T]hinking is at the root of doing and being' (p. 264) and this thinking is imaginative, critical, cyclical, open-minded, practical, dialogical, systematic and sympathetic. 'Clarifying the nature of our values, aims, and methods helps us to better grasp music educational beliefs and practices and understand self, other, and whatever lies beyond' (2011, p. 265):

> These pictures show us that every way of thinking or doing things has its unexpected consequences and detractions; when we encounter them, it is important to try to ameliorate the detractions, limitations and flaws wherever possible. (2011, p. 265).

Jorgensen's ideas about music education challenge us to look again at some of the models of music education which have been put forward as grand narratives or all-encompassing views of music education. Such models served a purpose of trying to capture everything taking place in music education, everywhere, for everyone and in every situation. While they can be useful as a way of simplifying complex ideas in terms that can be readily grasped and replicated, they cannot be used as fixed or static versions of music education. Metaphors, by contrast, 'can generate different interpretations of music education, along with divergent, inconsistent, and even conflicting ideas and practices' (p. 3).

Identifying issues concerning the selection of musical content in curriculum

Using England as an example we can address the way in which music education as a field of study presents music as a subject in the school curriculum. The National Curriculum sets out expectations for music education and states the purpose of a high-quality music education: 'to engage and inspire pupils to develop a love of music and their talent as musicians, and so increase their self-confidence, creativity and sense of achievement'. Note that the development of a love of music sits alongside the development of talent as musicians. Both are constructs originating in psychology and deserve careful consideration as they raise a number of issues about conceptions of value, selection of music and competence. They frame the way in which we approach how value is placed on music in the young child's life (and by whom), how music is selected for use with the young child (and by whom) and how notions of competence are ascribed for the child (and by whom).

In his review of how conceptions of 'children's music' have been presented in the literature, Panos Kanellopoulos (2008) outlines the psychological child as a product of developmental psychology, used to theorise about children's engagement with music in a simplistic way, and which created norms of behaviours from decontextualised practices. His criticism of this approach lies mainly in the lack of attention it paid to the context in which such practices take place:

> The intentions children bring to music-making, their perceptions of what composing or improvising is, the 'tool-kit' of strategies on which they might draw according to their prior experiences with improvising and composing, and the requirements of each situation in which they find themselves, are not issues worthy of attention. (pp. 220–1)

He suggests that a sociological approach to children's music practices would yield different sets of conceptions. Take, for example, a conception of the 'avant-garde child' which makes a connection between children's music and the creative processes that were used by avant-garde musicians of the 1960s, and the modernist aesthetic. Early proponents of this approach were Paynter and Aston (1970), Dennis (1970; 1975) and Murray Schafer (see Schafer, 1965; 1967; 1994). Kanellopoulos suggests that through this lens, 'children's music is seen as the prototype of experimental composition, of that stance of musical modernism that sought to do away with all reference to musical traditions, emphasizing innovation, while striving for unmediated personal expression and the achievement of new forms of musical unity' (p. 222). It was considered that children would come to discover the form for themselves, rather than using it as a starting point for their creativity. Kanellopoulos points out that a version of childhood such as this presents the child as tribal, acting in isolation. Yet the tribal child does not act in isolation. Music is not created in the head of individual children but in the dialogic space created through their participation in forms of music-making practices. Here the social and the individual dimensions are synthesised. 'In this approach, the "social" does not exist as a reified structuring system, but emerges through interactive meaning-making processes' (p. 225). In the next section, we will look at how conceptualisations of musical childhood are enacted in the formal education context.

Conceptualising musical childhood in education: England

Music education historian Gordon Cox (2015) uses examples from music education in formal educational settings to demonstrate the way in which childhood has been constructed over time, from the English medieval song schools, through instrumental instruction in eighteenth-century Britain, school music teaching in late nineteenth-century Europe, and to recapitulation and musical childhoods in the twentieth century. Cox argues that, while traces of all of these can be found in music educational thought, it is the fourth one – recapitulation – on which the concept of school curriculum is modelled, or, quoting Gould (1980), 'ontogeny recapitulates phylogeny' (Cox, 2015, p. 530). This is seen through an age and stage view whereby content is presented in curriculum or course of study, with a linear model of development where children progress through the system in years and come into contact with knowledge designed to bring about under-standing: '[I]n their embryonic development, individuals passed through stages similar to those through which their ancestors had evolved' (p. 406).

Cox shows how this maps onto phases of musical development. Drawing on articles written by Wilfrid Mellers (1964a; 1964b) for the *Musical Times* on the topic 'Music for 20th century children' he describes how Mellers (1964a) focused on a phase of 'magic and ritual' in the junior school. Predicated on a notion of the savage child, this phase is underpinned by a return to primitive intuition, where rhythm and a connection with the unconscious form a necessary and important foundation for all subsequent musi-cal development. He draws parallels between this corporeal encounter with rhythm and the musical worlds of composers beginning in the late nineteenth century with Wagner, Stravinsky and Bartok and taken up further by Varese, Partch, Cage and Feld-man in the 'New World' of the twentieth-century soundscapes, and found too in the 'Schulwerk' of Carl Orff where 'the mythology of the child's world of the rune and the nursery rhyme' (Mellers, 1964a, p. 344) has survived. What is interesting about Mellers' writing is the influence it had on the development of the creative music movement which grew up during the 1970s, championed most notably by John Paynter who was based in York at the time and whose classroom projects were offered to teachers as suggestions for lines of work and as gateways into creative music making (Paynter and Aston, 1970).

There are 36 projects in all and each one can stand on its own or be used in combi-nation with others. The authors are adamant that they do not constitute a 'method' of teaching music. Indeed this is to be avoided at all costs: 'We hope teachers will try to release the natural creativity in those they teach, whatever the age and ability of the pupils' (p. 23). The age range for which the projects might be suitable is deliberately wide though some might more easily lend themselves to one age group than another in terms of the topic. They want the children to realise that the music they make is part of the mainstream of human creative endeavour. Each project follows the same shape, with most having four sections, A–D.

Section A introduces the project. It outlines the principles behind whatever technique is to be discussed; it suggests the kind of background material we think will be needed by the pupils. This could form the basis of a short introductory talk before the class embark on the creative work itself.

Section B is the creative work in the form of an assignment or a series of graded assign-ments for a class, small groups, or individuals according to the nature of the material and techniques.

Section C contains examples of other people's working of one or more of the assignments. These are included only for guidance of teachers so that they may have some idea of what results to expect.

Section D is material for follow-up work, to include listening to the work of others and to learn how their projects and creative outputs have connections to the work of professional composers, particularly those active around the same time.

In their guidance, they suggest that there must be variety, and there must be an aim towards coherence of expression. Questions to ask are not 'Is this right or wrong? but Does this piece hang together? Does it "read as a whole?" Does it say what I want it to say? Is there anything in it which should be rejected because it destroys the wholeness of the music?' (see pp. 13–14). The responsibility for judging quality is as much with the creative pupil as it is with the teacher. They recognise the limitations of notation and taking their lead from composers who have found traditional notation inadequate they move to creating graphic systems or inventing their own notations. 'Notation is not music. The sound comes first. If children want to write their music down that may be the moment to teach some of the conventions but guard against the danger of killing the music's spontaneity' (p. 14).

At the same time as this was unfolding, a core curriculum was being trialled for young children at the primary school level. Under the directorship of Arnold Bentley and funded by the Schools Council, the aims and objectives of the core curriculum being proposed were to provide a progressive and systematic course which includes:

a. musical experience (both performance and 'creative') to provide the equivalent of spoken language experience before reading and writing begin
b. a music literacy progression with opportunity for individual rates of progress
c. a systematic building of musical concepts
d. a systematic programme of auditory and visual discrimination
e. a progressive development of vocal and motor skills
f. music of different periods and styles
g. words of songs etc. that are relevant to the child's stage of development and experience
h. musical material that it is possible to perform without the use of a piano [...]
i. a balance between creative, recreative (performance) and listening elements in the curriculum and between recreational activities (often reinforcers) and learning activities
j. music related to life (i.e. ordinary living) so that it does not appear as an isolated and exceptional phenomenon
k. a logical system of pitch development that would enable the teacher to use sol fa or letter names of notes or numbers (as in the Ward method), or a combination of these methods
l. clear stages of development to reach a plateau of achievement. If necessary more than one 'route' will be devised to reach each plateau. These 'routes' might be necessary because of different methods of teaching or because of individual children's rates of progress. (Schools Council/University of Reading, 1974, pp. 1–2)

Materials for teachers were devised and classified broadly into seven stages:

- Stage 1 for Reception infants (4-and-a-half years old+)
- Stages 1 and 2 for middle infants (5+ to 6+)
- Stages 1, 2 and 3 for top infants (6+ to 7+)
- Stages 1, 2, 3, 4 and 5 for lower juniors (7+ to 9+)
- Stages 1 to 7 for upper juniors (9+ to 11+) (p. 2)

Concept-building materials to support the early stages of music literacy were developed, which included terminology and music-specific vocabulary combined with a structure kit to help teachers who are 'initially musically illiterate' (Kendell, 1974, p. 3). Children were exposed to songs considered developmentally appropriate in terms of how music was presented structurally as moving from the simple to the complex using stage theories of musical development.

Rena Upitis (2019) reminds us of the limitation of a reliance on songs categorised as 'children's songs'. Not only do they assume a universality of appeal for children but they set up an expectation that music in childhood is about learning songs from others. 'We encourage children to play with language, with words – utterances but seldom encourage original musical utterances from children, referring them instead to listen to, replicate, or imitate the music of other composers' (Upitis, 2019, p. 22).

This points to an important paradox. In the primary school system, educating the young 'primitive' child has tended to be understood as training them in music literacy, tonality and song singing for the purpose of bringing about mastery in a narrow set of structured activities whereas the older child is given a free rein to express and from there to find the structure. In the first, the instruction starts with the symbols – the visual aid of notated music – and in teaching the young learner to read music, whereas in the second, the focus is on engaging with the sounds themselves, and from there moving to symbols, and encouraging the learner to create their own notations. For a detailed critique of music education in the UK during the Schools Council era, see Cox (2001). In the next section, we see how these two approaches were combined in the form of a national curriculum.

Music education in the school system

The introduction of a national curriculum towards the end of the twentieth century saw music included within the statutory framework of the education system for children from 5 to 14. It is presented as a form of knowledge which can be traced to Keith Swanwick and June Tillman's (1986) layering of sonority, expressive character, structural coherence and personal valuing in the school context. Music education is a developmental process underscoring the importance of performance, and of critical engagement with music as the foundation of composing, where children create music on their own and with others. At the earliest stages it is intended that children should be taught to experiment with, create, select and combine sounds using the inter-related dimensions of music. From there they are expected to develop an understanding of composition, exploring and manipulating ideas within musical structures and reproducing sound from aural memory. Composing and improvising to a specific brief (or range of purposes) is included. Learning is envisaged as incremental and ongoing, presented in key stages which facilitate the extension and development of musical ideas.

Each key stage represents fluid and focal points of engagement with 'knowing', which includes *knowing that* (propositional knowledge, informational knowledge and factual knowledge), *knowing how (*skills acquisition needed to produce or reproduce it) and *knowing by acquaintance*. It is in this third way that we can know music by engaging with it; by coming to know it like we would a friend (Swanwick, 1994).

More recently (Department for Education 2014; 2021c), the introduction of a statutory framework for the Early Years Foundation Stage sets the standard for the learning, development and care of children from birth to 5. It is relevant to all those who are involved in early childhood care and education, including state and privately run places, nurseries, homes and carers. Three characteristics of effective teaching and learning are identified:

- **Playing and exploring** – children investigate and experience things, and 'have a go'
- **Active learning** – children concentrate and keep on trying if they encounter difficulties, and enjoy achievements
- **Creating and thinking critically** – children have and develop their own ideas, make links between ideas, and develop strategies for doing things (2021, p. 16).

Seven areas of learning and development are identified, all of them interconnected. These are:

- Communication and Language
- Personal, Social and Emotional Development
- Physical Development
- Literacy
- Mathematics
- Understanding the World
- Expressive Arts and Design

The EYFS framework sets out characteristics of effective teaching and learning, but it is not prescriptive. As such the EYFS can be seen to offer us a watershed moment in [music] education. It offers each learning provider the freedom to adopt an approach to suit the circumstances within their particular setting, and to shape a learning environment which promotes their tastes, values and ethos. It is an opportunity to move away from a legacy where childhood is described as a preparatory stage in life, of becoming rather than of being. It has potential for rethinking the two distinct and contracting approaches to music education in the contemporary schooling system in England, and the narratives around them: one predicated on the implementation of a sequential programme of instruction, leading to music literacy in the early stages of a child's schooling (4+ to 11), with modes of assessment which measure attainment in discrete skills; the other project based, with creative endeavour designed to use sound and silence as a means of releasing children's so-called natural creativity.

Conclusion

In this chapter we have outlined some of the complexity around music education as a field of study. We explored Jorgensen's device of pictures to try to shed light on this complexity, and in doing so revealed some assumptions underpinning curriculum. Having recognised that the taken-for-grantedness of views can be challenged, we are compelled to ask ourselves how we come to make decisions regarding the selection and organisation of musical content in the educational context. This decision-making process is central to our understanding of music, both as a music maker and a music taker. It underpins everything about the way we approach music education.

It requires of us an awareness that our decisions are informed by the meaning and value we ascribe to music, and that they will impact on our capacity to provide experiences for learners which are authentic and relevant to their lives.

Reflection tasks

Consider the three vignettes presented below and identify how Jorgensen's models and metaphors might be helpful in describing the picture of music education being suggested in each one.

Vignette 1: Preparing for a choral festival

Fiona has been the music teacher in an all girls primary school set in an inner city area designated as disadvantaged. Soon after her arrival over 20 years ago she initiated a choir to provide her pupils with opportunities to travel outside their area and to take pride in themselves and their efforts. The choir is open to the older aged pupils (aged 9–11) and entrance is by audition. The music they sing is predominantly western classical music and differs from the music they grew up with, which she described as 'songs from the shows, stagey stuff … the music of the area'. She believes that she has lots to offer the children and wants them to 'hold their head up high and get a sense of the good'. She recalls an incident to show how the pupils themselves have bought into her musical world:

'We were working on the words especially the "t" at the end of the words and there was a girl in the front row who just wasn't getting it and I was getting her over and over to say it and somebody along the line was getting a bit fed up of listening to me so she said to the girl: "Lisa Jane!" she said, "you're sayin' it common, will you say it posh!" And the girl got the message straight away.' adapted from Stakelum (2008)

Vignette 2

Alan, aged six, moves stealthily around the classroom. He is the Wolf creeping out of the deep, dark forest. As he creeps he makes music: a pattern of mysterious taps and scraping sounds which tells us that the Wolf and the forest are sinister and fearful. No-one has instructed him: Alan chose the drum himself and decided himself how the Wolf's music should go. As he creeps slowly across the room, he is lost in the world of his imagination, intensified by the music he is making. (Paynter and Aston, 1970, p. 1)

Vignette 3: Earliest memories of playing music

'I started playing mbira when I was four years old … I grew up with mbira everywhere, in my house, in my home, in my village. My brothers were playing mbira, my father was a very good singer and mbira player the same as my mother... [W]hen you grow up in a village you are not just a child of your father and mother. Everybody in the village puts something in your being and your growing up so I'm a child of a village. That means all my education was based in being in this village.' (Interview with Chartwell Dutiro, 18 November 2015)

2

PERSPECTIVES ON MUSIC, MUSICALITY AND MUSICAL KNOWLEDGE

This chapter focuses on:

- Exploring the concept of music as art object
- Musicality as a discourse rooted in psychological tests and measures
- The emergence of musical competence as a psychometric construct and its legacy in music education
- Exploring the concept of musicking centred on relationships
- How these concepts interact with theories about music education
- Theories of musical development applied to education and the impact of this on children's musical worlds
- Contemporary perspectives on musicality and calls for inclusive learning environments

Introduction

In this chapter we begin with a philosophical perspective on the notion of music as a concept which uses sound as its defining characteristic. We contrast this with a suggestion that music is not an entity but a human activity with multifaceted dimensions. This human dimension is at the heart of the notion of music as a form of knowledge and raises interesting questions about meaning, form and value, and how they might be applied to music education. From there we explore how musicality as a discourse emerged from the field of psychology and led to a culture of testing which became an accepted way of defining and labelling children's musicality. This includes an examination of theories about learning and assessment and the way in which they have informed models of musical development. We chart the development of musicality in the young musician within the formal institutional settings and in the wider sociocultural context, where the term has become contested and challenged as a concept.

What is music?

We will use the definition applied by French musicologist Jean-Jacques Nattiez (1990) to explore the concept of music from a philosophical point of view (see his chapter 'The Concept of Music' for a full discussion). Nattiez uses a tripartite framework – the acoustic definition of sound, the perceptive approach and the compositional attitude – and applies it to the concert hall performance context where the focus is on the sounds themselves, and where typically the audience members listen in silence to the music being performed:

> a sonorous fact of any kind is recognised as music when we make the distinction between music and nonmusic … (p. 41)

Nattiez applied principles of semiotics to the concept of music and set out three conditions which needed to be satisfied in order for something to be counted as music. The first of these was to provide an acoustic definition of music as sound. The sound can be present or absent but it is a necessary component: '[W]e would not know how to speak of *music* without referring to sonority, *even when the reference is only implied*' (p. 43; italics in original). The second condition is concerned with the *perceptive*. By this he means that what matters is not whether the sound is heard or is implied but that it is perceived by the listener as music. This brings to mind Nattiez's third consideration, namely the compositional attitude where what matters is that the sounds are accepted as 'musical' by the composer. In other words, the sounds are accepted as 'musical' by the composer, although they might be rejected by the listener as noise. In the next section we explore this relationship between music as art object and what it can communicate.

Music as a language

In his influential book *The Language of Music*, Deryck Cooke (1959) proposes that music functions as a language, establishes the terms of its vocabulary and explains how these terms might be interpreted. Writing within the narrow frame of western classical tonal music, he takes pitch, time and volume as three dimensions and examines how they can function. Central to his thesis is that the tension between the dimensions is what conveys expression. Just as literature makes use of a language of sounds for the purpose of expression, he argues so too does music, though the expression is emotional expression. Unlike literature, which can utter abstract intellectual statements, the musically informed listener can recognise what is intended (see p. 25 for the analogy between literature and music). In this way, music is a language of the emotions. It explains how those who have a feeling for music but no technical knowledge can justifiably be said to 'understand' a piece of music. What is needed in order to understand music is simply to learn the grammar of music and obey its rules. By using this discursive logic it should be possible for us to explain music by referring to its constituent features, so that, for example a melody written in a minor key, or using descending minor third in the melodic contour, would indicate sadness in the music. Contrariwise, bright, shrill sounds would signify 'happy' sounds. Thus it can be possible to translate features in the music into their meanings, much the same way as a dictionary allows us to attribute a particular meaning to a word or phrase.

Others point out that although there are parallels in the way in which music and language have evolved over time, this does not suggest that they are the same. Henkjan Honing (2009) outlines the ways in which music and language differ. For one thing, whereas language can be divided into grammatical and non-grammatical structures, music cannot. It is possible for music to be understood as music even where rules are absent or unknown to the listener. Moreover, in addition to the lack of syntax music has no semantics. There are no labels which we can use to attribute meaning to music in the way that we can in language. Music appeals more directly to the emotions than language which acts as an intermediary. Finally, music cannot be captured in an alphabet as language can.

Michael Spitzer (2004) argues that since the emergence of the idea of music as a language back in the nineteenth century, we have been led to a paradox of reception history. 'In one respect, true understanding is indefinitely postponed, as we remain forever behind the work. On the other hand, we are in some respects actually in advance of the composer' (p. 320). We can examine or analyse the music, discern what we consider to be the thinking processes of the composer, compare the work of the composer with others sharing what we identify as common tendencies or innovative practices. Yet we must acknowledge that there is a limit to what we can actually understand of the composer's intentions or to answer for ourselves the question 'What does the music mean?'

Music and meaning

In his essay on musical meaning, Stephen Davies (2011) moves away from notions of musical meaning which focus on linguistic or semiological frameworks to argue for a broader perspective and, in doing so, singles out three types of musical meaning. These are formal musical meaning, experiential formal meaning and meaning-for-the-subject. He explains that the term 'formal meaning' is used to describe the specific properties of musical form. Malcolm Budd argues: 'the core of musical understanding – of hearing music with understanding – is the experience of what shall be called the intramusical meaning of a musical work, that is, the work's audible musical structure, the musically significant relations (melodic, harmonic, rhythmic, and so on) that obtain amongst the sounds and silences that compose the work' (1995, p. 127). Davies calls this the formal significance of musical ideas. He says that 'this type of meaning consists in the coherence of the structure of the work; to understand the musical work is to understand how it is put together' (p. 72).

In essence, what is being said here is that the meaning is to be found in the music itself (intramusical). This term has a resonance with Leonard Meyer's (1956) 'embodied meaning' (p. 35). Meyer used this to refer to the meaning which is held in the music itself. He contrasted this with extra-musical meaning or 'designative meaning':

> [a] stimulus may indicate events or consequences which are different from itself in kind, as when a word designates or points to an object or action which is not itself a word. Or a stimulus may indicate or imply events or consequences which are of the same kind as the stimulus itself, as when a dim light on the eastern horizon heralds the coming of day … The former type of meaning may be called designative, the latter embodied. (1956, p. 35)

An extension of this is experiential formal meaning where one understands a piece's formal musical meaning by appreciating the internal connectedness of its parts. Here Davies (2011) suggests that we do not need explanation or reasoning but simply the experience, as it is in our encounter with the music that our understanding is to be found.

> Music appears to have an experiential rather than a discursive logic. We do not merely perceive a succession of patterns in music. Instead, we experience the musical parts as connected into a dynamic whole. There is sense to the way music progresses. Music presents itself as a continuous process which, at every moment, what we hear follows in a compelling way from what came before; that is, music proceeds not as the temporal succession of otherwise unconnected elements but as the unfolding of an integrated whole. (2011, p. 75)

Davies gives his third perspective on the term 'meaning for the subject' and this is used to denote the way in which we associate music with events in our lives. The music reminds us of something. It can be an episode or activity in our lives, experienced individually, by ourselves, or collectively, shared with others. To illustrate this, he takes as an example the way in which music can have meaning for a group of teenagers who self-identify as members of a group (p. 83). Finally, there is the broader view of 'meaning for us'. This taps into the evolution of human species and the meaning or significance music has for humankind, forging empathy and communication with fellow human beings, as a social encounter.

Custom and practice of collective listening

A paradigm of listenership has grown up around this concept of music as art object. With its origins in the ideas of Eduard Hanslick (1854), it is predicated on a notion of absolutism, whereby music as [aesthetic] object can be presented for contemplation with reference to characteristics such as pulse, duration, dynamics, tempo, timbre, texture and structure. The concept of music as a work of art produced by a composer for consumption by an audience can be applied more readily to some contexts than others. In western classical music, for example, there has been considerable attention paid to the notion of music as a language of the emotions and from this perspective the listener needs to come to know what to listen for in the music being presented. Programme notes can explain or demystify the composer's intention, point out features and signpost the listener to sections or points of interest or significance: in effect they create a map of the musical journey for the listener and provide access to the music as art object. That the meaning of a piece can exist outside the music and can be explained to the listener in this way is founded on a belief that music functions as a language; that there is something to communicate, and that it is possible – and even desirable – to educate or inform the listener about what the music is about, what it tries to convey, what it means, and from there to deepen their understanding of the experience. Nor is it necessary for the members of the audience to know each other, to know the composer or the performers or indeed for them to have heard the music in advance. What matters is that the music is presented by the composer for performance as a completed work of art, and received by the audience as such.

The custom of collective listening in silence to music highlights the fact that the music is at the centre of the listening experience and of course it demands of the listener the capacity to be able to distinguish between music and nonmusic. We have seen that Nattiez was concerned with this in his concept of defining music. To illustrate this, he uses John Cage's *4'33"*, a piece which lasts for four minutes and thirty-three seconds, during which nothing is actually sounded by the performer. He explains that 'a silent work in which the pianist places his fingers on the keys and removes them again, repeatedly, without ever sounding a note' (p. 43) can qualify as a piece of music because the sounds or noises made by the audience constitute the music. This is exactly what Cage intended and is perhaps the most controversial and direct way of challenging the listener's perception of the boundaries between music and nonmusic. Regardless of the origin of the sound, or the variety of ways in which music is interpreted, it is this human dimension which matters in defining music.

We must keep in mind of course that the way in which music has been understood or accepted as music depends to an extent on how it aligns itself with the norms and tastes of its day. There are numerous examples of first night performances which led to uproar in the audience because the music appeared to contravene what counted to the listener as acceptable musical conventions. An example of how the reception history of a piece of music has changed over time can be found in Igor Stravinsky's *Rite of Spring*. The first performance première of this piece was held in the Théâtre des Champs-Elysées in Paris in 1913 and there are contemporary accounts of the riots it caused in the auditorium because the sounds presented in the piece were perceived by the listeners not as music but as noise. This changed over time and exposure to this same piece of music by today's audiences would no longer provoke such a strong negative response. It is a reminder of the changing tastes to music and the gradual shift in listener reception to music from rejection to acceptance.

Framed in this way, the listener has responsibility for defining what counts as music and where the border between music and noise lies. Nattiez holds that this distinction is culturally defined, and there is thus no definitive version of a piece of music: 'even within a single society, this border does not always pass through the same place: in short there is rarely a consensus' (1990, p. 48).

Emergence of a culture of testing in music education and its focus on measuring competence

In the early twentieth century, a culture of testing emerged which set out to identify norms in human behaviour. It originated in the field of experimental psychology where principles of scientific investigation were used to measure potential and achievement. When applied to music, the techniques of testing and measurement led to the practice of presenting musicality as a set of skills in discrete areas of behaviours, centred largely on the ability to pick out differences in short segments of sounds.

A pioneer of this approach was Carl Seashore, an American psychologist whose work on measuring musical talent appeared in 1919 (Seashore, 1919a; 1919b) is considered to be the earliest test in musical capacity. It was predicated on a theory of specifics, that is, where ability in music is understood as a genetically determined capacity, evidenced by a set of loosely related basic sensory discrimination skills.

According to Seashore, musical capacity may be divided into a number of sharply defined talents which are unrelated and can be present or absent in individuals in varying degrees. The focus in his battery of tests was to discern in the listener abilities in pitch, loudness, rhythm, time and timbre, and tonal memory. Although now over a 100 years old, the test is still in existence and has become hugely influential in promoting ways of weighing responses to musical stimuli as right or wrong. In a later work (1938) he appraises the procedures on which his initial work was based, noting that his use of the word 'measures' was deliberate: 'I adopted the term "measures" instead of the word "tests" in order to distinguish these experiments from the ordinary pencil and paper tests which deal with unanalyzed situations. The word "measures" implies standardized procedure in accordance with laboratory principles' (p. 303). See Julia Eklund Koza's (2021) analysis of how Seashore's work in testing and measuring human behaviour was founded on eugenics and set in place conditions which promoted an unhealthy separation of those destined to fail from those destined to succeed. Other ways of using tests as the basis of evidencing aural response to stimuli followed, including those created by Herbert Wing (1961), Arnold Bentley (1966), Edwin Gordon (1965; 1970) and Richard Colwell (1968). While each one differed in some respects, taken together they present a compelling justification for reinforcing a particular view of musicality, namely that it could be graded and standardised.

The presentation of musicality as a set of discrete, measurable behaviours can lead to the influencing of decisions concerning the organisation of learning in the classroom, the selection and content of musical knowledge in curriculum, and the manner in which progress is identified and measured. The test itself can become the focus of teaching, with a focus on product over process and an expectation that mastery is discernible to teachers and demonstrable by learners. Most of all, it facilitates the presentation of music as an art object, accessible through engagement as listener, composer or performer.

Changing rules, changing perspectives

A seminal figure in setting out an alternative way of looking at the 'rules of the game' is John Blacking ,English ethnomusicologist and social anthropologist (1976; 1987). He spent a prolonged period of time living among the Venda people in South Africa, studying the development and expression of its members' musical ability in the context of their social and cultural experience. He came to see that music played an important part in the life of the Venda, and his experience had a profound and lasting effect on the way he understood musicality. Prior to spending time with the Venda, his experience of music was that it involved repeated exposure to a narrow range of compositions, largely created between 1400 and 1953, and he understood music education as the acquisition of a repertoire of performing and composing techniques and musical values associated with this narrow field. This privileged art music over folk or traditional music. All of this contributed to a concept of music as artefact, a thing in itself devoid of the context within which it originated, and transmitted without regard to the social and cultural environment in which he grew up.

> Distinctions between the surface complexity of different musical styles and techniques do not tell us anything useful about the expressive purposes and power of music, or about the intellectual organization involved in its creation. (1976, p. vi)

Blacking's exposure to the music of the Venda caused him to reconsider his own views about music and musicality. He explains how he had been brought up 'to understand music as a system of ordering sound, in which a cumulative set of rules and an increasing range of permissible sound patterns had been invented and developed by Europeans who were considered to have had exceptional ability' (1976, p. vi). In this musical world, where the culture of testing had impacted on defining musicality and musical ability, he found himself pulled by two conflicting pressures in meeting the expectations of those with whom he came into contact. The first of these was to demonstrate technical accuracy in his performance and mastery of form in his compositions and the second was to demonstrate his awareness of the capacity for feeling. Blacking describes how this led to confusion at school:

> When I was at school, I found it very difficult to cope with this … confusion about form and feeling. My composition teacher complained that melodies which I had felt, lacked form and that those I constructed carefully were arid and unlovely. When he demanded accuracy in my performance and my grandmother complained that I practiced without feeling, I felt that both my technical skill and my integrity as a person were under attack. (1987, p. 73)

This separation of music making into two distinct components, one concerned with technical accuracy, the other with feeling, suggests some form of hierarchy where technical mastery was privileged, and 'feeling was some Teutonic quality that one added to music when one got the notes right' (p. 73).

In this regard, he cites the Seashore tests. The Seashore tests are based on discrimination of some kind but they are culturally specific to the western classical music system of intervals and scales. They are not universally applicable and must not be presented as such. 'Tests of musical ability are clearly relevant only to the cultures whose musical systems are similar to that of the tester' (1976, p. 6). But he calls into question their usefulness: 'what do the tests test, and how far is it related to *musical* ability?' (pp. 6–7; italics in original). He goes further: they may be useful as a means of recognising the intervals to be found in music and act as the foundation for translating these into an emotion, but this presupposes that there is a direct relationship between music and language, and that patterns of sounds can convey or signify a particular emotional state. (See p. 58 for a critique of Deryck Cooke's thesis on music as a language of the emotions.) Blacking asks: 'How useful are musical tests even within the cultural tradition in which they are set?' (p. 7).

It is important to remember that tests such as these emerged from experimental psychology. They were designed to be undertaken by individuals under laboratory conditions and carried out by a test administrator whose interest was the measurement of capacities or aptitudes in a narrow range of areas of musical behaviours. There was no relationship between the tester and the testee.

What is musicking?

We can look now at the ideas put forward by New Zealand-born sociologist and music educator Christopher Small (1998), who rejects the notion of music as a stable or fixed entity: 'music is not a thing at all but an activity, something that people do' (p. 2). In other words, music is not an artefact or abstract concept; nor does it take place in a vacuum. In order to distinguish this from the noun 'music', he offers a definition of the verb 'to music':

> to music is to take part, in any capacity, in a musical performance, whether by performing, by listening, by rehearsing or practicing, by providing material for performance (what is called composition), or by dancing. (p. 9)

It would include the activities of all those in the examples provided above, from the composer to the performer and to each member of the audience, all of whom Small considers to be engaged in some capacity with the activity of musicking:

> in using the verb *to music* ... we are reminded that all these different activities add up to a single event, whose nature is affected by the ways in which all of them are carried out ... [and] we begin to see a musical performance as an encounter between human beings that takes place through the medium of sounds organized in a specific way. (1998, p. 10)

What distinguishes his idea from that of Nattiez is the recognition that each encounter is shaped and influenced by the setting in which it takes place and the humans engaged in it. Small proposes a framework within which we can make sense of this, and underlines the importance for us to be aware of the part it plays in our lives.

> Everyone, whether aware of it or not, has what we can loosely call a theory of musicking, which is to say, an idea of what musicking is, of what it is not, and of the part it plays in our lives. (1998, p. 13)

A starting point for articulating our theory of musicking, according to Small, is to move away from asking questions of the music as object or artefact – what does this piece of music mean? – but asking ourselves 'the wider and more interesting question: "*what does it mean when this performance (of this work) takes place at this time, in this place, with these participants?*"' (p. 10; italics in original).

By moving away from a focus on looking for meaning in music, we can begin to see possibilities for considering ways in which our engagement with music can be meaningful. Here the context in which the musicking takes place and relationships between all those involved in musicking become central. These relationships

> are to be found not only between those organised sounds which are conventionally thought of as being the stuff of musical meaning but also between the people who are taking part, in whatever capacity, in the performance; and they model, or stand as metaphor for, ideal relationships as the participants in the performance imagine them to be: relationships between person and person, between individual and society, between humanity and the natural world and even perhaps the supernatural world. (p. 13)

Emergence of a culture of belonging in music education and its focus on developing meaningful relationships

The writings of Blacking and Small have had considerable influence on the way in which music educators think about musicality. For example, Thomas Turino (2008) sees great value in the relationships of those involved as participants, with everyone equal and where the emphasis is more on taking part than on presenting the art work. His ideas resonate with John Blacking's view that the value of music is to be found in the human experiences involved in the creation of music. Both of them make a distinction between 'music that is occasional and music that enhances human consciousness ... music that is simply for having and music that is for being' (Blacking, 1976, p. 50), with Blacking noting that 'the former may be good craftsmanship, but that the latter is art, no matter how simple or complex it sounds, and no matter under what circumstances it is produced' (p. 50).

Turino calls into question the prevalence of presentational music. By this he means music which is presented by a performer for an audience. He counters this with participative music where everyone is involved as equals and the emphasis is on taking part. In this latter definition, musicality is not identifiable as competence but as a human phenomenon. What matters is the connection made with others through participation. This notion resonates with Blacking's ideas, which are centred on the experience involved in its creation.

> [T]ying musicality or any ability to innate talent is a hindrance and can be used as an excuse for not participating in activities like dance, music, and sports that, due to their universality around the world, appear to be basic to being human. (2008, p. 99)

Turino argues that there is a oneness deriving from taking part in this, which he calls 'sonic bonding' (2008, p. 3). In this respect, he identifies four different traditions of music, noting that sonic bonding is more easily achievable in some rather than others. The first of these is the practice whereby music is presented by performers for an audience, which he defines as 'presentational music':

> Presentational music is a field involving one group of people (the artists) providing music for another (the audience) in which there is pronounced artist–audience separation within face-to-face situations. (pp. 51–52)

The experience of listening in audience fits neatly into this category and sets in motion a set of assumptions about the requirements for presentational music events. The audience has chosen to attend, has expectations about what is to be presented and accepts that their role is to listen in audience to the artists who have prepared carefully for the event. He contrasts this with participatory performance, which he defines as 'a special type of artistic practice in which there are no artist–audience distinctions, only participants and potential participants performing different roles' (p. 27). Here labels such as performer, listener and composer are not relevant but all are participants involved equally in what is resonant with Small's description of 'musicking'. Turino notes that the values underpinning participatory music traditions differ from those of presentational music traditions. 'Whereas presentational music is prepared by musician for others to listen to, participatory music is *not for listening apart from doing*' (p. 52; italics in original). Both presentational and participatory music making have to do with music performance in real time. He points also to the need to find ways of conceptualising music which is not produced in real time but exists in recordings and introduces two categories, namely high fidelity and studio audio art. The first of these is connected to live performance and involves techniques such as recording, sound engineering and production, roles which contribute to the creation of the recording. Studio audio art is not intended to represent real-time performance but 'involves the creation and manipulation of sounds in a studio or on a computer to create a recorded art object (a "sound sculpture")' (p. 27). Turino points to the fact that these four fields do not refer to one particular genre or style category but instead cut across the categories. He sees them as separate art forms with different potentials for human life. They provide tools for thinking about the processes, quality, value and potentials of different types of music making, each in its own terms (p. 89). Each one should be valued equally, and understood in terms of what it can offer to different types of people and in different types of situations. For example, participatory music has more in common with a 'good conversation' than it does with presentational music and the recorded forms. It can make artists of everyone, even the most reticent of us. It can offer opportunities for fun and social bonding. But it can come with constraints too, placing limits on individual creativity and experimentation. For its part, presentational music offers opportunities for challenging us to demonstrate our heightened abilities, allowing us to provide inspiration and enjoyment for others. It can generate anxiety however in certain circumstances and in certain types of individuals and as a consequence can change the experience for the performer and pose limitations on the number of people who choose to perform.

In the next section we take into account the people and the places in which music education occurs. We move away from a master–apprentice relationship where the purpose of music education is to transmit knowledge of music as art object, focusing on western art music, towards a model of education where what matters is the transformative nature of the encounter with music for all those engaged in it, learning alongside each other and the centrality of the context within which the music encounter takes place. Such a perspective can be found in critical pedagogy.

Critical pedagogy and the transformative purpose of music education

Critical pedagogy is based on a view that the purpose of education is not to amass knowledge or information but to transform the conditions in which we live. Originating with Paulo Freire, it begins with the social context, recognising that those who are involved in the teaching and learning encounter have a part to play in their own education. They are encouraged to assess and critique the content, the material – the prescribed curriculum – by becoming aware of the conditions that shape their lives and from there acting to take ownership of changing them. This conscientisation (Freire, 1970) or critical awareness and engagement (hooks, 1994, p. 14) blurs the distinction between teacher and learner as both work together to address the challenge or problem identified.

Freire likened education to a 'banking system', rooted in the notion that information can be consumed, deposited and stored for retrieval. His point is that the students articulate for themselves what they want or need to learn, informed by their view of the world and the problems they pose from the experiences they have had. Writing from her perspective on engaged pedagogy in a multicultural context, hooks (1994) notes that both teachers and learners are engaged in this transformation:

> [teachers] working to transform the curriculum so that it does not reflect biases or reinforce systems of domination are most often the individuals willing to take the risks that engaged pedagogy requires and to make their teaching practices a site of resistance. (p. 21)

Influenced by Freire's (1970) idea of conscientisation, Juliet Hess (2019) applies critical pedagogy principles to music education where the learner is central. The social context of the learner is taken into account and encourages young people to construct their knowledge through rigorous assessment of the material they encounter. This is an active learning process, entangled with empowerment and liberation. The focus is not on working within structured structures but in moving away from the tried and tested routines. Skills, knowledge and voices develop from engagement in the activity that is transformative (O' Neill, 2012), shifting the focus from performance to participation, from measuring individual endeavour towards celebrating belongingness, and which puts the context of learning at the heart of everything.

Conclusion

In this chapter we have looked at two different ways in which music education can been constructed. The purpose of this has been not to suggest a polarity or binary approach to music education but to highlight the importance of coming to know about music education by knowing how both 'music' and 'education' can be understood in many ways. Central to the first perspective was the concept of music as art object presented for aesthetic contemplation. This has its origins in a nineteenth-century notion about creation and reception in music, supported by practices of testing and measuring musical capacities rooted in experimental psychology of the early twentieth century. We can see how some of these ideas about music have found their way into the construction of music as a school subject. For example, we can recognise the practice whereby 'great' works of music are listed which are considered to be essential in every child's music education from an early age; exposure to, and familiarisation with these, 'the canon', is the mark of a good music education; music has meaning which can be accessed by coming to know the rules; and the role of the teacher is to support the learner in coming to know music by developing competence as listener, performer and composer. While learning to be a competent musician is one way in which a knowledge base for music education can be described, it is not the only way, and the purpose of including the second perspective was to explore this. The concept of music as something people do brings with it a set of rules which move away from a focus on competence as performer, listener and composer, and put the relationships between the participants at the centre. In this second perspective, knowledge is contingent, the consequence of cognitive and social interaction, with its meaning negotiated among the participants. Rules and their implementation are not enough but depend on the meaning of those rules particular to the individual situation, and on the experiences of those involved. This move from learning to be a competent musician to becoming a culturally competent one changes the nature of the knowledge base in a number of ways. Music making is a human experience often woven into daily life. The purpose is clear to all participants.

Reflection tasks

Consider the following scenario:

Imagine yourself as the teacher who plays a recording of a short excerpt from *Carnival of the Animals*. There are 30 children in the classroom, and the average age is 9. The children listen to the music in silence. When the listening excerpt has been played, the teacher asks them the following questions:

- How does the music make you feel?
- What can you tell me about the piece of music you heard?
- Describe what is going on in the music.
- Draw a picture of the animal you imagine.

There are a number of assumptions lying behind the teacher's choice of music. Can you identify them?

Consider each question posed by the teacher in turn. What set of beliefs about music education underpins each one? Is there a link between this set of beliefs and the meaning and value music holds for the learners? What learning is likely to take place?

3

MUSICAL IMAGINATION IN THOUGHT AND PRACTICE

In this chapter we will explore:

- the notion of imagination as a human capacity related to thinking and doing in music
- links between music, imagination and play
- children's engagement with musical imagination
- reimagining perspectives on music and its relationship with the world

Introduction

In this chapter we look at the concept of imagination from a variety of perspectives. Beginning with a reference to philosophers in Ancient Greece we track thinking on the topic in more recent times, including that coming from within the arts, and within music specifically where play is a central feature. We relate this to play in children's musical worlds and consider the relationship between education and the development of musical imagination in practice. In pointing to the tensions inherent in imagining the future and [re]imagining the past we conclude that it is not just education but the boundaries between music and nonmusic that need to be reimagined.

Exploring imagination

One of the distinguishing features of being human is the capacity to imagine. With varying degrees of vividness, we can imagine the face and touch of a loved one, for example, or the sound of a car horn, or even the smell and taste of our favourite food. What links all of these is a connection between our conscious experience of holding the image in mind and the conscious experience associated with perceiving that particular stimulus in the real world (Pearson, 2007). Not only does the concept of imagination concern itself with mental imagery, human development, theory of mind, counterfactual thinking and creativity both separately and together (Roth, 2007), but it reaches across a wide range of disciplines including philosophy, psychology, musicology, palaeoanthropology and language. This means that, while the term is readily used in everyday life, finding one all-encompassing definition of imagination as a construct is quite a challenge.

Philosophers have been engaged in the study of imagination as a form of knowledge for a long time, and we can trace back at least as far as Plato's theory of ideas to distinguish the notion of 'image' from an object that is knowable and truly real (Kenny, 2010, p. 45) and Aristotle's theorising on sensation to distinguish between objects that are particular, such as colour, sound, taste and smell, and those that are perceptible by more than one sense (motion, number, shape and size). He recognises other faculties which later came to be grouped together as the 'inner senses, notably imagination (phantasia) and memory' (see Kenny, p. 194). Socrates began to ask about the purpose of a thing: he considered that it was this, and not only its description, that imbued it with value. There is not the space to examine these ideas in any great depth here, apart from noting that they can be seen to reappear in various guises over the years, and in epistemological terms, prepare the ground for questions about the purpose of [music] education.

In seventeenth-century thinking, French philosopher René Descartes distinguished between a passive image-forming faculty and a semi-active power of recombining what is sensed, and English philosopher Thomas Hobbes expanded on this to identify two types of imagination. The first he called simple imagination or fancy, which is brought about by a sensory movement. When this movement of the sense ends, the image or 'phantasm' remains and as it decays it is called memory. To this he adds compound imagination, which is the capacity for us to combine two images to form another:

> when, from the sight of a man at one time, and of a horse at another, we conceive in our mind a Centaur. (Elements of Philosophy IV, xxv; in Beardsley, 1975, p. 171)

What is interesting here is that it is in this compound imagination that novelty is to be found. The nineteenth-century fascination with the imagination is well documented too, and as Beardsley (1975) observes, it was when the Romantic theorists began to foreground connections between inner senses such as intuition and insight with a gift or ability to participate feelingfully, that imagination extended from the inner life of other human beings to the inner life of the world itself (American philosopher of art, Monroe Beardsley, 1975, p. 253). 'It was the claim to this form of knowledge that gave rise to a new theory of the imagination – or, perhaps better, that was not only a faculty of inventing and reassembling materials, but a faculty of seizing directly upon important truth' (p. 253). It was this truth which was considered to be a quality of beauty. This fusion of creation and cognition was a legacy of the Romantic poets and can be seen to influence aesthetic theories about symbolic thought across other arts, including music.

Music and imagination

In his writing on music and the imagination, American composer Aaron Copland (1952) suggests that of all the arts, 'music provides the broadest possible vista for the imagination since it is the freest, the most abstract, the least fettered of the arts: no story content, no pictorial representation, no regularity of meter, no strict limitation of frame need hamper the intuitive functioning of the imaginative mind' (p. 7). Yet, as musicologist Nicholas Cook observes, there is no 'theory of musical imagination' (2007, p. 123), although conceding that there is increasing consensus that it relates to thinking and doing. Anecdotally, we find Mozart often used as an example of how imagining operates in the world of music. Details of how he could bring to mind the inner workings of his imaginings and commit them to paper fully formed are sometimes used to demonstrate how the mind of a musical genius works. What is interesting is the material expression and documentation of what has been imagined. For Mozart it was the production of a complete work. There is evidence of his mental imagery in composition to be found in his letter where he recounts how he hears the parts all at once and later recalls these, committing to paper what he has held in his memory (see Vernon, 1970, p. 55). In the context of music performance, Terry Clark et al. (2012) point out that the capacity for musicians to engage in mental imagery extends beyond imagining the sounds to simulating the physical movements required to create sounds, a 'view' of the score or an instrument, and the emotion a musician intends to convey in the music. They recommend that mental imagery should be seen as an integral part of practice, and just as hearing is important to the musician, so too should musical experience be considered a multisensory one, and rehearsed through mental imagery to create a vivid and realistic experience that can closely resemble the actual activity.

Within the field of psychology, theories of mental imagery are used to explain how the mind appears to be able to simulate or re-create sensory-like experiences. This can vary from person to person but it remains the case that we use this faculty in everyday life and across all senses. The capacity for children to imagine is said to be particularly in evidence as they engage in 'make believe' and 'play', attributing objects with imaginative properties, and there are theories of its development across the lifespan. In the next section we will look at ways in which imagination is connected to play and in doing this we will explore ways in which imagination can be developed in the child.

Play world and worldplay

Robert Root-Bernstein (2013) distinguishes between play worlds and *worldplay*, explaining that the latter refers to "the repeated evocation of a fully realized imaginary place often (but not always) inhabited by imagined beings engaged in imagined behaviours or characterized by imagined systems within some imaginary culture" (p. 417). The worldplay is not transitory but persistent and of personal significance to the one imagining, and is governed by an ability in the child to be able to hold both the world of the plausible and the fantastic. Finally it involves narrative growth and system building.

As we noted earlier in respect of Mozart, much attention has been paid to documenting the imagination of the prodigy but little was known about the way in which this worldplay works more broadly, for the normally developing imagination, until the work of Robert Silvey and Stephen Mackeith (see Silvey and Mackeith 1988), which led to a set of criteria characterising invented worlds. They termed these worlds paracosms and were intent on moving away from a focus on the extraordinary or precocious intellect on the one hand and pathologies indicative of mental illness or distress on the other. They preferred instead to focus on a key component, namely an awareness of and ability to recognise the difference between make-believe and real-world thinking: in other words, the capacity for 'as is' and 'as if' thinking.

. Root-Bernstein identifies three ways in which worldplay can contribute to the development of imagination, moving from a world 'as is' to a world 'as if'. At the start is the notion of play as pretence. Pretending involves make-believe, where the child has an opportunity to adjust their 'as is' reality to work within an imagined world framed by pretend stipulations, by causal principles that motivate pretend behaviours and actions, by the suspension of objective truth in favour of make-believe truth and by an unfolding chain of linked events (Harris, 2000). This playworld can persist throughout childhood. A second facet is the role of inventiveness, using what is at hand or known and refashioning it or tinkering with it to create something new. It involves blending and modifying ideas, what Stephen Nachmanovitch (1990) calls bricolage, or a tinkering with and re-purposing of materials at hand. This tinkering might involve 'thinkering' (Root-Bernstein, 2013, p. 426), or a tinkering in imagination only. An important point to note is that unconventional thinking is not the only measure of vigorous imagination. 'The blends that surprise us also reveal hidden likenesses and relationships between hith-erto unconnected things' (p. 426). This brings us to the third component, that of model-ling, where the rules, though made up by the individual, are plausible enough to relate to some generalisable or shared understanding. In other words, it must be possible for the creator to document what they have created in their imagined world. Without this there is only internal reverie or daydreaming. This holds for the teacher and the learner: the story itself can act as a bridge between the world of the child and that of the adult.

Music, imagination and play

Mary Reichling (1997) explores the ways in which music, imagination and play work together and separately in play and musical experience. She names four in all, the first of which she calls fantasy, make-believe and magic. This is where children – and adults – can envisage or bring to mind things that do not exist, regardless of how realistic or life-like they may be. Performers will recognise it in the way they might make present an idea they bring from the music they play, an idea which is imagined but helps them to bring the music to life. The listener can imagine something in the music that they see as vivid, a representation of a character, a feeling or an event that is evoked in the music. Some-times the composer of the piece might be complicit in this, and we will see examples of this in Chapter 4 with Saint-Saëns' images in *Carnival of the Animals* and Prokofiev's *Peter and the Wolf*, where a melody can take on the image of a character in the story. As Reichling reminds us, these images and characters do not actually exist but are brought to life through the imagination.

A second facet identified by Reichling is that of fantasy where the imagination works to make present things that do exist in the real world but are absent from the person at the time of imagining. Take for example the activity of calling to mind a favourite song. It is not being played in real time but is known to the listener and can be remembered. This act of inner hearing is available generally and in educational terms has been used to particular effect by educators such as Zoltan Kodály in systematic ways using an audio-visual schematic strategy to develop an intelligent ear, summarised as 'seeing what you hear and hearing what you see' (see Chapter 4). It is known too to be useful in sight read-ing, where what is required is the capacity to be able to hear silently what is presented in visual form before it is made audible.

In addition to fantasy imagination, Reichling shows how a third facet, namely that of figurative imagination, can function as play: 'this phase of imaginative activity is often described as "seeing as", or aspect perception, that is, imagining X as Y, where Y is a rec-ognisable aspect of X'. In the case of music, figurative imagination comes into play when connected to feeling. The listener can respond to the music by interpreting what is heard as invoking or evoking a particular feeling, can experience the music as 'sad', 'joyful' or some other emotional response. These feelings are metaphoric however and not real, and the examples provided by Reichling underline the need to remember that the feelings felt by the composer when writing the music are not directly transferred on to those felt by the listener when listening to the music. The fourth facet is literal, which operates in perception and recognition of symbols, notations and rules which govern the practices related to music. There are also spatio-temporal considerations, the illusion of time and space, the movement through time and space, and the illusion too of the ascending and descending patterns, all of which need imaginative thinking to grasp: 'Interpretation occurs along the continuum of imagination from fantasy to recognition and between subjective and objective spatio-temporal considerations' (p. 52).

A number of researchers have applied the notion of musical imagination to thinking differently or thinking outside the box. David Zerull (1993) presented a framework of musical imagination which had six different functions: perception, sensing, memory, synthesising, judgement and experiential. Of the six, he considered the experiential function the one with higher-order functions leading to something new. Robert Dunn (1997) refers to creative listening as a particular type of listening which involves both objective and subjective responses. These responses are active and involve 'thinking in sound' and reflection-in-action – that is, perceiving the music as it happens, creating expectations of what may happen, reflecting on what has happened, and interacting affectively with these perceptions (p. 45). Following Peter Webster (1987) he suggests that analysis plays a key part in this. By responding to the internal structuring of the music – recognising the patterns, the elements, the genre and so on – the listener can become a co-creator of the musical experience through an active process of understanding and explicating sound structures in written, verbal or mental form. One of the ways in which musical imagination can be shared is by representing it such that it can be accessed by someone other than the one who is imagining.

Educationalist Jerome Bruner (1966) has identified three systems by which we represent knowledge. The first, enactive, is about action. The second, iconic, depends on sensory organisation and on the use of summarising images and the third is symbolic in nature, where something is presented to stand for something absent. Bruner concludes that the heart of the educational process lies in finding ways to connect experience with systems of notation ordering; 'any theory of development must be linked both to a theory of knowledge and to a theory of instruction, or be doomed to triviality' (p. 21). In putting forward his theory of instruction he wants to focus on how to *improve* and not simply to describe learning. There are four major features required:

a) creating the conditions conducive to learning under which the learner can be willing and able to learn;

b) presenting knowledge in ways that are most readily grasped by the learner – personalised learning;

c) the sequence or unfolding of the content; and attention to reward for learning – how will the learner know that they have learned and to what extent can the learning move towards self-sufficiency; and

d) independence, where the teacher becomes redundant.

Bruner's belief that 'there is nothing more central to a discipline than its way of thinking' (1966, p. 154) has been applied to music education in a number of ways. We see it underpinning a view of musical thinking as a way of defining knowledge. In respect of early childhood music education, for example, Laura Huhtinen-Hildén and Jessica Pitt (2018) illustrate how a story such as *Moominvalley in November* by Tove Jansson can provide a structured pathway to enter and explore this imaginative musical and arts world (see p. 170f). They take a thematic approach to making music visible and tangible and identify fascination and caring as the cornerstones of their pedagogy. Their concern is with the nurturing of the inner artist and the creation of learning environments through imagination. 'Through the process of adventure in story, we can inhabit the art form (music-story) to gain deep insight and learn musical aspects from within" rather than being "taught" from the outside' (p. 170). This allows the learner to 'search for their own music' (p. 171) and recasts the relationship between 'teacher' and 'learner'. In this musical world, the boundaries are blurred and all are-co-learners.

Engaging [with] the child's musical imagination

In the field of music education, many published schemes of work include pieces of music which are chosen for the purpose of guided listening. Typically these pieces have been given titles by the composers which evoke some response or set up expectations about a possible story or narrative. In her account of the way in which music listening became legitimised in textbooks found in the American school system, overtaking the music appreciation movement which was so prevalent in the earlier part of the twentieth century, Rebecca Rinsema (2018) points to a tendency in the authors to privilege a particular way of listening which she terms 'an engagement hierarchy' (p. 484). By encouraging listeners to engage with music in a certain way – as concert listeners – she argues, there is still a privileging of western classical music practices, or what she calls a 'stylistic hierarchy' (p. 484). Attentive listening, active listening and structural listening have in common a singular focus of attention on the music and the music alone. She wants us to go beyond this and to look at other ways of engaging with music, so that the concept of listening to music is inclusive and enables us to theorise contemporary music listening practices and what their relationship might be to the classroom today (p. 486). We can do this by taking a hermeneutic posture or a meaning-oriented posture, where the meanings might be different for people in different contexts. She calls for a 'robust, pluralistic theory of music listening and music meaning for the classroom, one that does not focus on just one way to listen and one that does not rely on or reinforce universal hierarchies' (p. 488).

There are a number of important points to pick up on here. The first is to identify what a universal hierarchy means in the context of music education. It involves selecting music that the teacher considers to be of value, and what every child should become familiar with. It means playing recordings of the music and asking children to respond to its formal characteristics, or asking them how the music makes them feel. It involves asking the children to represent it in extra-musical ways, perhaps by drawing a picture or writing a story or poem about the feelings or mood evoked through the listening. It could be argued that these are activities where music is a stimulus or catalyst for something outside the music itself. It reinforces the solitary nature of the experience and the concept that responses to music can be collected in isolated ways. It also uses the music being presented as artefact, and as object with a mode of communication between child and music mediated by the teacher. It is a scenario that will be familiar to anyone who has had music appreciation classes or who has been exposed to listening to music classes.

Yet the listening experience does not have to be just an individual or private one. It can be a socially shared activity where more than one imagining mind is engaged in 'what if' ways of thinking. This point is made by Tuuri and Peltola (2019) in their exploration of how we, as human beings, build worlds together with sounds and music. They report on a case study where two groups of three or four people listened to short music and soundscape samples together and discussed them afterwards. Their findings show that group activities such as this can act as a faculty for producing original content as well as reproducing a version of what they heard:

> [These group discussions on listening] concerned reciprocally a *perception* [italics in original] of the listened samples, as well as a *creation* [italics in original] of something new in terms of the possible ways of imagining these sonic experiences. This was evident in the negotiation processes, where typically individual group members picked up, and elaborated on, certain inspirational vocabulary, ideas and concepts from the other members' expressions (Tuuri and Peltola 2014). Consequentially, the exchange of such information helped individuals to rediscover and reimagine their experience, while also providing opportunities for reflectively validating the appropriateness of these ideas in terms of one's own listening experiences. The joint engagement in a group provided a basis to both shared imagining and the imagining of individual members. (p. 351)

Sound worlds or atmospheres such as these become extended and inclusive ways of listening and when applied to the educational setting they can be democratic multidimensional spaces of learning, along the lines promoted above by Rinsema. These dimensional spaces can extend beyond and outside a particular musical tradition and with developments in technology they offer potential for providing new tools for social interaction. Thus, sounds can be listened to *as if* they were music – not only in the sense that they would create melodic lines or rhythmic patterns similar to music, but also as temporal, sonic material for imagining and embodied experience (p. 352). In this way, socially extended imagining with sounds and music builds both collective and individual sonic worlds. For extensions of these ideas, see Schafer (1994), Westerkamp (2007) and Ceraso (2018).

Another outlet for musical imagination is the area of composing. Within the formal education sector in England, composing has been presented as one of the tripartite ways of knowing by acquaintance and we can trace this to the work of Keith Swanwick and Joyce Tillman whose model (see Swanwick, 1988) was predicated on Bruner's enactive, iconic and symbolic systems of presenting knowledge and Jean Piaget's emphasis on imaginative play. In Piaget's (1952) four- stage theory of cognitive development, he had set out how, in the early stages, play was a multi-sensory experience for children, involving their exploration of the immediate environment. From there the child's curiosity extends outwards, towards inventiveness and asking 'what if?' questions. In the third stage, children can begin to make connections, and find relationships between things. By the fourth stage, the children have the ability to hypothesise, to imagine connections in the abstract and begin to work flexibly within systems of thought. (For earlier examples of its application to researching musical development) in young children see Pflederer (1964), Zimmerman (1970) and Serafine (1980).

As an aside, it is worth mentioning that Bruner cautions against interpreting the contribution made by Piaget as psychological, and argues instead that it is epistemological, or 'concerned with the nature of knowledge per se, knowledge as it exists at different points in the development of the child' (1966, p. 7). Bruner considers Piaget's description of stages not to be explanations of the processes of growth but to relate to the nature of the knowledge that the child shows at each stage of their development.

The Swanwick and Tillman model was groundbreaking in its day. It grew from analysis of compositions of hundreds of young children, with each output created by the young children in response to a musical or extra-musical stimulus set by an adult. The children worked individually and thus we cannot extrapolate from their findings that this sequence of musical development holds for children engaged in group composition. Yet this collaborative interaction is increasingly being found to be important in education. Not only does it show that working in groups can facilitate improvement in all its members – the whole is greater than the sum of its parts – it acknowledges that learning does not take part in a vacuum but is influenced by a range of interrelated factors. Models such as that put forward by Swanwick and Tillman are not designed to be used as a shortcut to finding evidence of demonstrable growth in children's learning, or a means by which to determine musical behaviours in children, such that only those behaviours that we can define as `musical' are counted as valuable learning experiences. There is a temptation for the Swanwick and Tillman model to be used as an end in itself, where an over emphasis on meeting the descriptors set out in each of the dimensions of musical understanding can lead to a standardisation of knowledge. There is a danger too that, without fully understanding the rationale underpinning the model, the spontaneity and serendipity of children's learning might be overlooked, or interpreted as uninformed or unimaginative activity.

While much has been written about individual responses to music in the schooling context, and to performance by individuals, and to evaluating the output of imagination, very little is known about the group or community setting, at least not in the young child context. There is a lot of research on how this works in practice with adults (see Lave and Wenger (1991) for a discussion on communities of practice). Karen Littleton and Neil Mercer (2012) explore how musicians negotiate a collective 'sound'. They draw on talk and music as modes of communication for joint activity and frame their research within the sociocultural tradition, 'which sees creative processes as dynamic, fundamentally social and necessarily collective and collaborative' (p. 234). They note that, whereas much of what is presented in school practice has been based on a Piagetian concept of knowledge, with norms of human activity identified from observation of the behaviours of individuals, in the sociocultural tradition human activity gets its validation or affirmation from the group. This means that knowledge is shared and people jointly construct understandings of shared practice. From this sociocultural perspective 'humans are seen as creatures who have a unique capacity for communication and whose lives are normally led within groups, communities, and societies based on shared "ways with words" ways of thinking, social practices, and tools for getting things done' (p. 234). Their idea of group work is that it is collaborative, and that the members are partners in the group. In addition to the interaction that takes place within such groups, they point out that we 'interthink'. Using the example of music, they suggest that the talking, the conversation and the discussion are part of a multimodal toolkit for thinking collectively and shaped by the practice of each community.

In his work into the inner auditory worlds of children on the autistic spectrum, Adam Ockelford points to a fascination among some of them with sound apparently for its own sake. In other words, they do not separate the sound perceptual qualities from their function. This means that they can listen intently and intensively to sounds and appreciate their pattern and predictability. In coming to this understanding, he observes that early in life 'neurotypical' human infants learn to differentiate between auditory input according to one of three functions it can fulfil. These are 'everyday' listening (slamming door, carhorns), 'musical' listening (attending to qualities such as pitch and loudness) and 'linguistic' listening (based on the perception and cognition of speech sounds). While there is some debate about which of these develops first, Ockelford's view is that what makes music 'music' requires the capacity to be able to copy sounds. In other words, 'for music to exist in the mind, there must be *perceived imitation* of one feature of a sound by another' (Ockelford, 2019, p. 411). He sets out his ideas in a zygonic theory (Ockelford, 2013), which was developed from evidence 'that certain sounds, especially those that are particularly pleasing to an individual … acquire little or no functional significance for some children. Instead they tend to be processed only in terms of their sounding qualities – that is, in musical terms. It seems also that everyday sounds that involve repetition or regularity (such as the beeping of a microwave) may be processed in music-*structural* terms. 'There are many possible interpretations of the responses but what seems to be common is the interest in structure, and the intensity with which they can perceive, remember and imagine sounds can be explained to some extent by their heightened sense of remembering pitches with accuracy, their ability for absolute pitch and their love of pattern can offer possibilities for emancipating their auditory imaginations: and to do this 'through the capacity to understand musical structure and the rules of the generative grammars through which melodies, harmonic sequences, and rhythms are created afresh' (Ockelford, 2019, p. 424).

Suzanne Burton (2021) outlines the advantages and disadvantages of digital play and offers guidelines on how to evaluate the usefulness of apps designed for early childhood music education. She shows how traditional and digital play can combine to form converged play, creating new possibilities for children's engagement with music. 'As a different way to play, technology in early childhood music can maximize, support, supplement and extend music play' (p. 19). She lists the ways in which apps can offer children a different way to play:

- Physical locomotor play
- Vocal, language, or word play
- Exploratory play
- Constructive play
- Pretend, fantasy, and sociodramatic play

and notes that mobile technology has become part of the fabric of the society in which we live.

Imagining a soundworld that does not yet exist

With advances in technology there is greater possibility for reimagining ways of presenting sounds that exist and imagining sounds that do not yet exist. Trevor Wishart (1996) identified pitch- level and rhythm as two features of sound used in tenth-century western musical practice which 'appeared most accessible to analytic musical notation' (p. 22) and which have contributed to our understanding of the structure and structuring of sounds themselves (p. 4). He uses the concept of a lattice to show how the plotting of sound along the dimensions of pitch and duration, with pitch on one side and duration on the other, has conditioned and shaped our perceptions of sound. He points out that it was only in the twentieth century, with the development of technology, when the parameters of sound extended beyond what could be achieved by conventional instrument design – keys, holes and frets – that the limitations of notation became apparent, as did the term 'music' itself, which was seen to restrict itself to covering only those sounds which were associated with a source or cause. It led to the concept of sound-object, which could be analysed 'for its intrinsic acoustic properties and not in relation to the instrument or physical cause which brought it into being' (p. 129). With developments such as these, it became possible to engage with sounds in new ways, and to create soundscapes which did not depend on established customs and practices.

Simon Emmerson (2011) notes a shift in emphasis from music information technology to music *imagination* technology (my italics) and suggests that the digital computer allows infinite possibilities for the generation of sounds and sound sources. He defines imagination as 'the faculty or action of forming new ideas, or images or concepts of external objects not present to the senses' (2019, p. 260). He wants us to separate 'image' and 'imagination' as he believes the image tends to be limited to a visual component – what we can see – whereas imagination allows us to take into account a range of components from a range of elements – sensory, space and time elements. 'So, as musicians we may imagine a scenario, an instrument, a performance, a sense of space, place and movement, a form, an atmosphere' (p. 261). While these may not be *sounding*, they will provide us with a context for sound.

Reimagining relationships between music and the world

Recent discussions in new materialism are leading to new ways of establishing an understanding the role and place of us as humans and our relationship with the world. Some writers call for a move away from anthropocentrism, noting that the human capacity for thinking or reasoning has dominated discussions about the world for too long, and there needs to be a recognition that there are other – non-human – perspectives to take into account when considering how the world can be shaped and developed. As humans, we have grown up in a world based on rational thinking, with an infrastructure based on numbers and codes, which as Salomé Voegelin (2019 p.561) argues 'always and unavoidably are the design of a human-thought world'. Her interest is in reimagining the way in which materials – and in particular sound materials – can connect and work together to form a conception of the world as a relational field. In this reading, Voegelin (2019) suggests that 'sound is not "this" or "that" but is *the between of them*' (p. 560; my italics). By looking at the [musical] world in this way, we can see that nothing is fixed or anchored. There is no definitive version of a thing but multiple possibilities of engaging with it and imagining it. Everything remains fluid and uncertain, 'not necessarily as precarity, as a state of anxious fragility, but as a serendipitous collaboration between the multiplicities of the "what is"' (p. 561).

Placing uncertainty at the heart of the [music] educational process has implications for the way in which we conceptualise [music] teaching and learning. '[It]makes appreciable other possibilities of how things might be and how things might relate, and serves to consider positions and positionings of materials, subjects, and objects in a different and more mobile light' (p. 561). It invites us to look at the soundworld in new and unimagined ways, and to develop a sonic sensibility in ourselves and others. According to Voegelin (2019), a sonic materialism

> foregrounds personal responsibility and participation: not to deny our being in the world and the world being for us what it is through our being in it, but to embrace the human ability to think this position as relative rather than central; to appreciate our responsibility in how the world is: politically, ecologically, and socially; and to initiate change and a different attitude. (p. 561)

Let's explore this in relation to the teaching and learning context. Where the teacher as adult has had a longer experience of being in the world, their relationship with the sonic world is framed by looking at music as it is; that is, as sounds organised in accordance to rules and materials arranged in a particular way. Where this is recognisable as something known and familiar to the adult, it can be understood as 'good music' and selected for inclusion in the teaching tools for the learner, as something to pass on to the learner. There is evidence of this in a particular way in the 'canon' described in many curriculum documents. What the new materialists would say is that this view calls to mind a view of 'music' as culturally entrenched within a tonal system which is so much part of the sound world that we think of it as 'natural' or 'the way things are'. We see this in the sound sources too: instruments are tuned in one particular way and with timbres or tone colours arranged in families (broad categories such as strings, wind, brass and percussion). What if this were reimagined so that this sound world had a different reference point, where these structured structures (of sonic possibilities) were no longer acting as structuring structures? What might the sonic sensibility offer? Here the young learner has less to unlearn than the adult teacher. What is needed is a culturally responsive approach to music education, where the teacher and learner engage in co-learning, cooperating on the sounds to form new creations. It necessitates moving away from the closing off of sounds, vibrations, noises external to the sounds at the centre of the experience. For example it eradicates the need for 'concentrated listening to' music presented for contemplation. This places the listener within the music, and not outside it attending to it as object or thing. It brings to mind the example of the mathematics lesson in Chapter 1, where the young learner's response to the task set by the beginning teacher was not what was expected. We might argue that the situation required unlearning on the part of the teacher in order for her fully to appreciate the delight of the young learner. Moments such as these have potential to challenge some of the ideas put forward in curriculum documents about forms of knowledge, and invite us to reflect on what is possible in the classroom context when we imagine the world of learning from a child's perspective.

At this point we can look again at Vignette 2 presented in Chapter 1:

Alan, aged six, moves stealthily around the classroom. He is the Wolf creeping out of the deep, dark forest. As he moves he makes music: a pattern of mysterious taps and scraping sound which tells us that the Wolf and the forest are sinister and fearful. No-one has instructed him: Alan chose the drum himself and decided himself how the Wolf's music should go. As he creeps slowly across the room, he is lost in the world of his imagination, intensified by the music he is making. (Paynter and Aston, 1970, p. 1)

The scene being described is provided as an example of how education can be alive with the excitement of discovery, with exploring music as part of the wide field of human experience (1970, p. 3), and with moving away from re-creative towards creative activities (p. 6). From a research perspective, we could say that there is no evidence that Alan is imagining what the observers claim however: and therein lies one of the limitations activities such as this pose for the practitioner. Nonetheless, there is an important point to make about the vignette and it is this: the opportunity to explore is provided to Alan where he decides what/how/where to be in the space. A conscious effort has been made to remove the boundaries between school subjects so that what matters is space for exploring. With their classroom projects in creative music, Paynter and Aston (1970) set out to bring the notion of experimentation to the fore, so that the child learns by doing, and by working with the musical materials can come to know them and their possibilities. In this respect, they considered sound and silence to be central. By being in the world of his imagination, Alan has the capacity to explore the musical materials, to act on them and to develop new ways of knowing himself and his relationship with his environment.

Yet there is much that is omitted in the vignette. We do not know the background to the activity or why the activity takes place in a classroom setting. We have no information about Alan or the instructions or motivation for the activity. We do not know who else is in the classroom. We do not hear his perspective on the purpose of the activity. We can only imagine what is happening through the eyes of the authors: they observe his movements and they interpret his intentions.

Leaving aside the fact that this is probably an idealised version of music making and set against the background of its day, we can recognise that the scene being conjured up is an effort to reimagine classroom music as a way of countering the hegemony of music education rooted in experimental psychology, with an emphasis on trying to understand how humans process sounds presented to them for concentrated attention. The vignette invites us to consider how we might focus our attention on developing new forms of knowledge rather than on recreating (mastering) old or tried and tested ones.

Conclusion

One of the limits of working on one's own is that the activity can become isolated and lodged within the individual. The ideas never get shared with others. Finding ways to communicate with others about these musical imaginations involves negotiating, sharing and working as a group, ideally where each member of the group is there as both an individual and also as a member of the group.

In hindsight we must acknowledge that the efforts made by Paynter and Aston to create an experimental learning ecology did not go far enough in creating a viable alternative to the learning ecology of the classroom. There are challenges to overcome, not least in countering a perception that 'anything goes' or that there is no attention to (or need for) quality. What is needed is a reimagining of the learning, and of the role of the actors and a move away from the structures on which the teaching and learning have been built. What is needed is a learning ecology that reimagines the relationship between teacher and learner, where, as Peter Woods notes '[t]he definition of learning … shifts away from a process of collecting and engaging knowledge into a means of engaging and building community' (Woods, 2019, p. 462).

Following Woods (2019), we can see two independent themes emerging. One has to do with exposure to experimental music as pedagogy and the other is concerned with the interaction with objects/instruments. Experimental music offers an opportunity for music educators to consider the full range of musical forms that intentionally break from, or never involve themselves with, aspects of western classical music such as dimensions of pitch relations and synchronised rhythms (see Small and Walser, 1996). It allows us to challenge the foundations of western classical music (including the distinction between composer and performer (Woods, 2019)). Because there is no history, learning and co-learning become central. Presenting the teacher as expert is no longer appropriate because by its nature the work is experimental – there are no certainties.

Reflection tasks

There are many ways to define [music] education. Here are two that we found in this chapter:

a. 'democratic multidimensional space of learning' and
b. 'a serendipitous collaboration between the multiplicities of "what is"'.

How might each of these relate to your experience of music education?

4

MUSICAL WORLDS CREATED FOR CHILDREN

This chapter focuses on:

- Identifying adult conceptions of musical childhood
- Using a listenership paradigm to introduce children to 'the classics'
- Music written for pedagogical purposes
- Impact of these on music education

Introduction

This chapter is organised in three sections. The first of these features the practice in music education of using classical music that delineates a story or narrative to introduce children to principles of listenership. The second section provides an overview of the contribution made by the composer educators Zoltan Kodály and Carl Orff to children's music education, notably through the application of principles of play attributed to children's singing and rhyme. The third section examines the application of these principles in practice, identifies some of the commonly held assumptions about children's musical lore which underpin them, and considers the impact that adult conceptions of children's musical worlds have had on presenting approaches to music education and to children's encounters with music as universal.

Music delineating a story or narrative targeted at children

A number of pieces of music from the western classical tradition have found their way into textbooks presented as music appreciation opportunities for school-going children to the extent that they could be referred to as classics in music education. One such example is *Carnival of the Animals*. This was initially intended for a private audience, as a fun piece, and the titles might indicate this.

- 'Introduction and Royal March of the Lion'
- 'Hens and Roosters'
- 'Wild Donkeys Swift Animals'
- 'Tortoises'
- 'The Elephant'
- 'Kangaroos'
- 'Aquarium'
- 'Characters with Long Ears'
- 'The Cuckoo in the Depths of the Woods'
- 'Aviary'
- 'Pianists'
- 'Fossils'
- 'The Swan'
- 'Finale'

The piece was written by French composer Camille Saint-Saëns as far back as 1886 and it continues to be held up as an example of music suitable for use with children in classroom music lessons. Take for example the recently launched Model Music Curriculum (Department for Education, 2021b, p. 64), which includes it in a list of music for listening. In trying to understand how a piece of music such as this has endured in the education system, we could point to the fact that the composer used a framework of a carnival or circus within which each of the short pieces can be given its own title. This makes it easy for the listener to identify where each piece fits within the overall scheme of things. We can see too how the theme of animals might be seen to have appeal to young children, with each scene lending itself easily to being translated into visual representations or interpretive accounts. It becomes accessible to teachers too who can give instructions such as 'imagine the swan gliding across the water' or 'describe in words how you think the spectators felt when waiting for the carnival to begin'. A further point to consider is that each segment or piece lasts a short length of time and the teacher can be fairly confident that the learners will have the concentration span necessary to sustain them through a hearing of the piece. Taken together, these factors present an attractive package to the classroom teacher, and indeed to publishers, as an ideal conduit through which the aesthetic properties of instrumental music can be supported or, some might argue, supplanted by the associative properties evoked in the listener. By following the instructions and exercises provided in textbooks on listening to music in the classroom, teachers and learners can explore together the musical world contained within the pieces and use them as a springboard for extended activities. An approach such as this, where a piece of music is selected for a specific purpose, is commonplace in music education in the institutional context. We see it in the model music curriculum (p.18), where 'The Elephant' from *Carnival of the Animals* is used to inform the developing of listenership in the young learner, with particular reference to identifying sound properties in isolation.

The relationship between story and music

Another example which has found its way into the classroom is a symphonic fairy tale, *Peter and the Wolf*. Unlike *Carnival of the Animals*, which was written for adults, *Peter and the Wolf* was a commission specifically for children and composed by Soviet composer Sergei Prokofiev in 1936. Prokofiev adapted a folktale as the basis of his music, assigning specific orchestral instruments to characters in the story and thereby introducing a musical device called leitmotif or leading motif, common in works of the time. Listeners to this music can respond to the drama unfolding in the story, recognise the musical instruments being played and remind themselves of the characterisation and plot. In contrast to Saint-Saëns, who gave instructions that his work was not to be published in his lifetime, Prokofiev was keen to inform the audience and it is said that before each performance of Prokofiev's piece the themes were introduced to the audience on the instruments:

> Each character of this tale is represented by a corresponding instrument in the orchestra: the bird by a flute, the duck by an oboe, the cat by a clarinet playing staccato in a low register, the grandfather by a bassoon, the wolf by three horns, Peter by the string quartet, the shooting of the hunters by the kettle drums and the bass drum. Before an orchestral performance it is desirable to show these instruments to the children and to play

on them the corresponding leitmotivs. Thereby the children learn to distinguish the sonorities of the instruments during the performance of this tale. (Morrison, 2009, pp. 46–7)

Whereas *Carnival of the Animals* was not designed for educational purposes, *Peter and the Wolf* was, and we can see how Prokofiev used a storyline to introduce the musical world of the orchestra to the young listener: his intention was to make visual and audio connections possible as an accompaniment to dramatic events as they unfolded in the music.

In each of these pieces of music, it is possible to ask 'what does the music mean?' and to get a response. In the case of the first, the title of each piece gives us the strongest clue but when combined with the sound sources used we can conjure up the composer's intention with a greater degree of certainty. For instance, the title 'Fossils' makes sense to us when we associate the timbre or tone colour of the instruments chosen to represent skeletons dancing so that a visual image comes to mind. We do not need to know the names of the instrument but we would need to cognise (*cognere* = to know) what a fossil is before we can recognise (come to know again) what the music is conveying to us or represents something of the fossil to us. The capacity for us to hold these in our mind at the same time as we listen to the music allows us to begin to 'understand' the music as it is presented to us in real time. When we recognise how the piece `Elephant' has been devised to portray an animal who is heavy and likely to struggle with applying four feet to the steps of a dance such as the waltz (where steps are in groups of three), a situation compounded by the juxtaposition of light piano sounds and heavy double bass sounds, we can get an insight into the `musical joke' intended by the composer or the humour infused into the piece. Thus it is possible for this piece to work on a number of levels. We must ask ourselves on which level does the child operate and when the joke has been heard how many hearings will it sustain? 'The Swan' is a further case in point. In this case the image being portrayed is of a graceful elegant swan gliding across the water. There is an assumption of course that we have seen a swan. If we have never seen a swan, what might our relationship be to this piece? Will it mean anything? These are questions for us to consider when weighing up the value and purpose of such activities.

When pieces such as these are dominant to the extent that they become part of the musical canon in school, it is easy to overlook that they present only one musical sound-world and it is important to remind ourselves that there are alternatives to a sound palette firmly rooted in the western classical orchestral tradition. One example is *The Phoenix of Persia*, a book based on a story from the Iranian epic poem 'The Shahnameh' (The Book of Kings), written by Abolqasem Ferdowsi (940–1020 CE), with original music composed by contemporary Iranian musicians and performed on Iranian instruments set to the narration of the ancient tale. Each instrument is associated with a different character in the story. The music was performed on ney, qanan, tanbur, daff and santur. The music was created over a period of several months in the summer of 2018 by a group of Iranian musicians working collaboratively and with the storyteller. The storyteller and the musicians work together to relate the story and the music provides an accompaniment to the words being spoken.

Each of the pieces demonstrates the usefulness of storylines as an organising principle, lending themselves to descriptions or interpretations beyond the music itself, through pictures imagined, explanatory notes about the action, or idealised national attributes. Saint-Saëns' use of titles provides an explanatory framework within which the music can be interpreted and understood, though the piece was aimed primarily at adults and not at children so many of the allusions are unlikely to be picked up' by the young listener. Prokofiev's depiction of the grandfather in his piece was intended to bring to children's attention the attributes of an idealised version of Russian character, though it is unlikely that this is a prerequisite for listening as what has prevailed is the unfolding of the folktale through music. Just as *Peter and the Wolf* has a message about strength and courage, the message in *The Phoenix of Persia* is about forgiveness: 'Being human is being able to forgive'.

Music devised to introduce young people to the orchestra

Unlike the pieces mentioned earlier, where some of the sounds or sonic events within the music are associated with or refer to something outside it, Benjamin Britten's *Young Person's Guide to the Orchestra* relies not on a story or extramusical association but on the sounds themselves, unfolding as they do in a real-time performance context. Written in 1945, the piece was Britten's response to a commission for music to be used for educational purposes, and was targeted explicitly at introducing children to the orchestra and from there to classical music. He uses a pre-existing tune or theme from a piece by English composer Henry Purcell dating from the mid-seventeenth century. This tune is presented at the beginning and then in various colours, though always recognisable. Instead of using leitmotif as the organisational device, he used a tune as the binding force in the piece.

Whilst Britten uses the symphony orchestra as his sound palette and constructs the piece around variations and a fugue on a theme of Purcell, his intention is for the listener to attend to the sounds and discern the theme in its many iterations, and from there to develop a sense of the distinct character of each sound source or instrument on which the theme is heard. The focus of the listener is firmly on the tune or melody and how it varies each time it appears. Repeated listenings will increase the familiarity and allow for transfer of the sound quality from the tunes heard in the piece to other contexts. Ideally this would be accompanied by exposure to, or direct acquaintance with the instruments themselves – the sound sources – and though it may not be practicable or feasible to achieve this, the title suggests it was written for the specific purpose of introducing the young listener to the musical world of orchestral sounds. The music is intended to be listened to without the need for translation or interpretation such as that found in the pieces discussed earlier: it stands on its own. Imogen Holst notes the enthusiasm that permeates Britten's music from start to finish and how, although it becomes quite complex and multi-layered, it never falls into over-intellectualisation (1952, p. 279). She notes too that he has never fallen into the error of writing for children as if their language were different from his own.

> When Britten writes music for young people to sing or listen to, he is fortunately unaware of the school-teacher's habit of classifying human beings into separate age-groups … He has obviously never thought of youth as a 'problem' demanding special measures in education: the Young Person for whom he wrote his Guide to the Orchestra might just as well have been eight or eighteen or eighty. (p. 276)

The earliest published work in which Britten made use of children's voices was in the *Three Two-Part Songs* (1952) for boys', or women's, voices and piano. Children's voices also appeared in his score to the GPO Film Unit's *H.P.O. or the 6d Telegram* (an abstract film by Donald Taylor, produced by Lotte Reiniger in 1939). Britten's biblically themed *Noye's Fludde* was primarily intended for children and the set of songs *Friday Afternoons* was written for small boys to sing at school, with frequent use of repetition, which as Holst notes is the result not just of the practical need for simplicity and economy but a knowledge that 'children have an insatiable appetite for repetition and that they will seize hold of it' (p. 279).

Application to practice

Let's look again at the reflective task posed in Chapter 2 which asked you to consider a classroom scenario on listening to music.

> Imagine yourself as the teacher who plays a recording of a short excerpt from *Carnival of the Animals*. There are 30 children in the classroom, and the average age is 9. The children listen to the music in silence. When the listening excerpt has been played, the teacher asks them the following questions:
>
> • How does the music make you feel?
> • What can you tell me about the piece of music you heard?
> • Describe what is going on in the music.
> • Draw a picture of the animal you imagine.
>
> There are a number of assumptions lying behind the teacher's choice of music. Can you identify them?
>
> Consider each question posed by the teacher in turn. What set of beliefs about music education underpins each one? Is there a link between this set of beliefs and the meaning and value music holds for the learners? What learning is likely to take place?

The first point to notice is that the listening experience takes place in a classroom setting with 30 children sitting in silence. Music is presented as an artefact, which is invisible and intangible and can be accessed only by listening in silence. While we are told that they are aged around 9, we learn nothing further about them. We might reasonably expect that there is a multitude of personalities, interest and experiences represented in the classroom. We might also imagine that they will each have their own preferences and musical tastes outside school. Perhaps some of them have formed friendship groups based on common musical interests. In other words, they do not appear in the classroom as empty vessels to be filled with information, but a number of factors are likely to contribute to their preparedness for what is to unfold in the lesson. Because of the way in which the exercise is set up as a group activity, none of this appears to matter: the teacher designs how the encounter is to unfold. We can surmise that the music selected will dominate in the lesson but we learn nothing about the reasons behind the selection of this particular piece of music for this particular set of children.

It is only when we pause to reflect – and to make the familiar strange – that we can ask these questions and notice these gaps, and their significance, in the story.

In order to interpret what is going on, draw on the notion of a listenership paradigm introduced in Chapter 2 to consider the implications of this practice for the young musician and their relationship with music. In this piece of music, the sound sources are presented by an adult – the teacher – as opportunities for concentrated listening. The music is invisible, nonverbal and transcends the sociocultural context of its origin and reception. Framed in this way, we can see that the listening experience is not dependent upon a particular time, place or sociocultural context.

Next we consider the act of listening itself. Though conducted in a classroom populated by 30 children, the listening is private and solitary and silent. The teacher knows how long to expect the experience to last but it might be challenging to convey to the children the duration in words. They know that their silence is required until the music stops and this may well impact on the concentration they apply to the listening experience. For some this might invoke anxiety, for others boredom – what is certain is that no two children will have the same experience or response to the music being presented. However, because the situation is set up so that the teacher directs the lesson, there is limited insight available to us (and to the teacher) into the reception of the music by each individual child in the classroom. The method being used to gauge the response is through teacher-initiated questions.

Finally, we turn our attention to the questions posed. Let us now look at the first one: How does the music make you feel?

In this question, there is an assumption that music can make the listener feel something, and that this effect brought about by the music can be identified as such by the listener and described to the teacher. In the classroom context, where the music is presented for concentrated listening, and heard in a vacuum, responses to the music presented are framed without reference to the world outside the classroom, but in terms of discrete emotional states, typically organised as either categories or dimensions (Kreutz et al., 2006, 2007). Of the categories, the predominant emotional states expressed in music have been identified as happiness and sadness with a distinction made between valence (negative to positive) and arousal (low to high) as two orthogonal psychology dimensions (see Kreutz et al., 2007). In respect of the question being posed, there is a need to distinguish between what a listener perceives in the music and the effect the music has on the listener (Gabrielsson, 2002; Lundqvist et al., 2009).

While in theory, we might argue that it is possible to distinguish between each of these, in practice this distinction is not always clear. It is probably impossible to avoid allowing emotions, actions and behaviours to influence responses to music and there is no guarantee that listeners will block off the world outside music during the listening experience. Furthermore, this practice whereby each musical feature or emotional state is isolated by the listener, teacher or researcher for particular attention may be said to be governed by a set of assumptions: that each musical feature or emotional state can exist in discrete form; that each construct has a logic which is known to the researcher and can be recognised by the respondents; and that listeners will focus only on the musical stimulus with little interference from external factors. In addition, where the use of forced-choice responses may succeed in focusing the listener on a particular aspect of the music, it makes the listening process somewhat simplistic, 'obscuring the fact that the musical expression or portrayal of an emotion is fraught with difficulties' (London, 2002, p. 23).

Having weighed up the extent to which music can bring about an effect on a listener, we must surely contest the notion that our feelings exist in isolation and we can never say with certainty there is a direct relationship between the music being listened to and the corresponding feeling/s which emerge. To try to put this into perspective, how might we respond to a learner who says, in response to the question 'How does the music make you feel?', 'It makes me feel hungry, teacher'. My intention here is to demonstrate how complex – and simplistic – such a question can be, and to point to the importance of knowing what purpose it serves.

A more accessible, and interesting, question to ask (should questions be needed) is the second one: What can you tell me about the piece of music you heard? This question does not pinpoint feelings but rather invites a diverse set of responses which may draw on dimensions of knowledge other than aesthetic knowing.

The third question, Describe what is going on in the music, has potential to elicit some imaginative responses but it must be remembered that it depends on recall and remembering 'what is going on' before formulating a response.

The fourth question is perhaps the most commonly used, which is Draw a picture of the animal you imagine. Here the music is used as a stimulus for a nonmusical or extra-musical response. We do not know whether the teacher told the children in advance that the music denoted a swan. Notwithstanding this, there appears to be an expectation that the music conveys something about an animal and that this is awaiting discovery. One way of gaining access to this is through images and words, and there are numerous examples of research that demonstrates how this can be done. In her effort to unpack some of the complexity around gaining access to children's listening to 'Jimbo's Lullaby', a piece of music planned, designed and intended for children, Rivka Elkoshi (2015) undertook a study with children (n = 209) aged between 4.0 and 9.5 years and within their grade groups. There were eight groups in all, and in each case the data collection was organised over the course of a class of 45 minutes, with four hearings of the music presented. After the second hearing, the participants were asked to express their impressions verbally and these were audio recorded. After the third hearing, they were asked to graphically create a drawing that they considered to represent the music. A fourth hearing provided an opportunity for them to complete their drawing. These hearings were undertaken in a classroom encounter and all participants could hear their responses and see the graphic responses. Individual interviews were held after this to allow for further exploring of the responses with each child and further description and explanation of how the drawing related to the music. Elkoshi found three categories of response: A – associative, F – formal and C – a combination. She found a prevalence of A responses over F responses, which suggested to her that children were capable of perceiving and responding to the global attributes of the music – drawing on their subjective experiences and intuitive use of a range of symbols. They were less inclined to attend to musical characteristics and the children drew their responses to the music and she interpreted these, differentiating between age groups. Her study was based on a recognition that, although the music may be for children, it is not childish or simple. It is of course important to remember that the study was undertaken in a school setting under conditions set up by an adult (the researcher) who took responsibility for selecting the piece of music to be presented, and the manner in which the responses would be documented and reported. What is not known is how the young participants would have chosen to listen to the music if left to their own devices or indeed whether it would form part of their listening preference outside of school.

Activities such as these within the formal school context remind us that there is still a residue of the laboratory conditions under which testing took place in the early part of the twentieth century. Much remains unknown about the musical worlds of children in the informal out-of-school context. Judy Lewis (2020) argues that musical engagement is a cross-modal experience, involving more than the aural and with too much emphasis placed on 'what' is listened to: '[a]t the root of this perspective is the notion that listening is fortification for – in service of – higher level music performance skills rather than an engagement in its own right' (p. 374). She notes, with Randall Allsup (2015), the prevalence of a teacher-directed structure [in schools] that favours learner obedience' (2015, p. 13). She incorporates a communal aspect of meaning making into her study alongside the individual. In other words, learner preference is taken into account and forms the basis of open-ended encounters with music, encounters that are fuelled by the learners' own inquiry and imagination, their own questions, wonders, and problems posed' (Lewis, 2020, p. 383).

Critiques such as this invite us to reappraise the relevance of introducing pieces such as Saint-Saëns' *Carnival of the Animals* to young children in a twenty-first-century music education context. What is needed is 'a profound reorientation' (Kress, 2010, p. 79) where 'new questions emerge [and] old questions get recast' (p. 15). Lewis considers this to be an exciting opportunity for music education, which starts with music teacher educators who embrace new literacies, new ways of situating music education. 'By doing so, we situate music education as a uniquely central component in the broader global educational project of twenty first century literacies' (2020, p. 385).

In the next section we consider the contribution of adult composers to the music education of young children. We pay particular attention to Zoltan Kodály and Carl Orff, both of whom have published music for children, and whose influence can be seen in approaches to music learning that are still in existence today.

Graded pieces constructed for pedagogical purposes

Zoltan Kodály and the musical mother tongue

Kodály's belief that music belongs to everyone grew from his experience of Hungary as a nation where music was valued as a status symbol (Kodály, 1974) with little relevance to the culture and tradition of the Hungarian people. He was critical of songs which were taught to young children, arguing that he could find no 'authority to judge from an artistic point of view the songs that are to be taught' (p. 142). Along with the absence of musical value he found them to be harmful from a pedagogical aspect too (p. 142). 'The texts [in use] do not start from the soul of the child and his [sic] view of the world but impose upon him the author's own "self", and this "self" is not a poetic individuality … but a kindergarten "Auntie", a pedagogue … [who] view[s] the child from without, describe[s] what the child is doing and make[s] him sing it while performing it'. He was scathing about the materials in use at the time. As Katalin Forrai (1988) summarised: 'The music education of a people must begin with its own folk traditions. It is only through the small musical forms that world masterpieces can be approached. Only music of artistic value can serve as musical material' (p. 13). Kodály envisaged a musical world within which children would be exposed to their musical mother tongue from the earliest opportunity. Singing would be a foundational activity, and the role of folksong should be central in music education, and the selection and organisation of musical material according to specific age-groups. Only when a child can read music can s/he begin to learn a musical instrument.

The Kodály concept was built on the simultaneous development of '[a] cultured ear, a cultured intellect, a cultured heart and cultured fingers' (Szönyi, 1983, p. 17; see also Nemes, 2017). He drew on Guido d'Arezzo's hymn 'Ut queant laxis' for sol-fa. Written in the eleventh century, the first syllable of each line contains the sol-fa syllables (ut re mi fa sol la). The handsigns devised by John Curwen (1816–1880) allowed the singer to visualise the pitch and removed the barriers put in place by a dependency on notation. Émile-Joseph-Maurice Cheve (1804–1864) had introduced a system for rhythm names. Kodály combined all three – solfa, handsigns and rhythm names – in his pedagogical approach, giving children access to musical material which was graded, and tuned predominantly to pentatonic sounds of the Hungarian folksong tradition. Beginning with the descending minor third (s m), the young child learns to sing a repertoire which is Hungarian. Numerous examples can be found in his publications for children.

Between 1937 and 1967 he wrote compositions with a pedagogical purpose:

1937 *Bicinia Hungarica, Volume I* (two-part exercises)
1941 *Let Us Sing Correctly*
1941 *15 Two-Part Singing Exercises*
1941 *Bicinia Hungarica, Volumes II, III*
1942 *Bicinia Hungarica, Volume IV*
1943 *333 Reading Exercises*
1944 *Pentatonic Music, Volume I*
1946 *24 Little Canons on the Black Keys*
1947 *Pentatonic Music, Volumes II, III, IV*
1954 *55, 44, 33 Two-Part Singing Exercises*
1954 *Tricinia (Three-Part Exercises)*
1954 *Epigrammes*
1962 *50 Nursery Songs*
1963 *66 Two-Part Singing Exercises*
1965 *22 Two-Part Singing Exercises*
1967 *77 Two-Part Singing Exercises*

His volume '*333 Reading Exercises*' contains many of the tunes and others which are idiomatic: 'each is excellently suited to the teaching of melody and rhythm to small children, serving additionally as a solid foundation in acquiring the Hungarian vernacular' (Szönyi, 1983, p. 35). Through immersing themselves in this graded sequential approach to learning, children become familiar with and tuned to structure, form and harmony. By a systematic method of drill and rote learning, the child would internalise what they heard and learn to hear internally. This principle of inner hearing has become a cornerstone of Kodály's legacy and shaped the way in which music literacy would be defined. For Kodály, the early start was vital: 'Basic training missed in youth cannot be made up for later on' (Kodály, 2007, p. 198). The role of the teacher was central to the success of the learner and the standard required of the teacher was high: 'as a general rule, only someone who has been taught well can teach well... How can we teach what we do not know ourselves? (p. 197). For Kodály there was room only for masterpieces, and by this he meant folksongs and then music of the masters. This cannot be left to chance, however, but was the duty of the school. As Blacking notes of Kodály, 'the role of music in educating the nation was to be achieved by dedicated, self-conscious performance practice, which cultivated the potential of individual and social bodies' (1987, p. 143).

Kodály's corpus of music written for children assumed that they would grow to appreciate their national music, and with increased exposure and training would become musicians of high quality. There were moves to replicate his ideas elsewhere and the principles of solfa were transplanted to other cultures, and applied to learning folksongs of many countries with varying degrees of success. We can see Kodály's work through the lens of national identity and in developing a sense of cultural pride in the music of the people. When seen within the context of its time, within a Europe that was conflicted and unsettled, Kodály's concern for education in and through music was closely related to the development of a community which was distinctly Hungarian. Blacking draws similarity between the ideals of Kodály and those of Australian-born American composer Percy Grainger. Both were interested in community but saw the role of music within it differently. For Kodály it was Hungarian and for Grainger it was the world (for an extension of this, see Blacking, 1987, p. 144).

Carl Orff and *Schulwerk*

Like Kodály, Carl Orff is associated with music for children and his ideas have been taken up internationally, most notably through the published work *Schulwerk*. He was careful to point out that this was not a fixed method or system of instruction: 'every phase of *Schulwerk* will always provide stimulation for new independent growth: therefore it is never conclusive and settled, but always developing, always growing, always flowing' (reported in Haselbach, 2011, p. 178).

Orff noted from his observations of children's musical play that it is often combined with language or dance but while music, movement and language are integrated, they differ too. Nor is it designed to a formula – or by taking a building blocks approach – but is an experience that first allows the child to turn towards music. He believed that the original encounter between human and music is its characteristic, and this is active, practical, with every attempt made to lead from hearing and making music to thinking and imagining. Perhaps the most widely known area is the instrumental dimension. He added a rhythmic-metric component to the singing of a melody. Communicative interaction is an important feature of elemental music education with a social dimension brought about when children listen, sing and play together. Finally there is a framework within which improvisation takes place, thereby facilitating the exploration beyond the boundaries while recognising them as boundaries.

We have seen how Kodály considered it important for children to have strong foundations in music of their own musical culture at the earliest opportunity. Songs and games based on pentatonic and diatonic systems formed the basis of this training. By immersing themselves in this musical world, he believed that they would fully grasp their musical mother tongue and only then should they take on the music of other cultures. Like Kodály, Orff starts with first principles, though he came to this through the cuckoo call in nature and not from an analysis of folksongs. He introduced the concept of elemental music, a term used to denote that it was near the earth, natural, physical, within the range of everyone to learn it and to experience it, and suitable for the child. Orff's vision of elemental music is captured in the speech he made in 1963 at a conference in Salzburg on Orff-Schulwerk in the School:

Elemental music is never music alone but forms a unity with movement, dance and speech. It is music that one makes oneself, in which one takes part not as a listener but as a participant. It is unsophisticated, employs no big forms and no big architectural structures, and it uses small sequence forms, ostinato and rondo. (Haselbach, 2011, p. 144)

The concept of always developing, always growing, always flowing is explored by Hermann Regner in his evaluation of the educational ideas underpinning Orff's approach. He summarises the learning activity as attitudes or behaviours that should be internalised in young children through music education. These are:

1. Turning towards music (motivation)
2. Discovering music (exploration)
3. Perceiving and experiencing music (sensitisation)
4. Making music (psycho-motoric techniques)
5. Understanding music (structuring)

All are closely related and overlap. In framing the contribution of Orff's educational ideas between utopia and reality, Regner points to the key role played by teachers:

whether Orff's educational ideas will continue to be an actuality, whether the clairvoyant anticipation of the future can be brought to life, this will depend on the ability, the understanding, and the determination of the teachers continuously to rearrange the ideas, in new ways in practical work with children. (Haselbach, 2011, p. 192)

What is distinctive about Orff's *Schulwerk*, he argues, is that it seeks to lay the foundation for a musical attitude, one 'that allows the individual and the social group to realise themselves, to affirm themselves in musical interaction, to live in music' (p. 192).

A universalist perspective on music for children

Both Kodály and Orff recognised the importance of music and childhood, and by observation and analysis of children's songs, each in his own way searched for universals underlying children's playlore. A universalist perspective of music has grown up around some of the practices based on rhythmic and melodic patterns and has become pervasive to the extent that it is sometimes presented as applicable to all children everywhere. This is problematic on a number of levels.

First, the concept of a universal rhythm in children's songs has been called into question by Blacking and others such as, for example Kathy Marsh, who cautions against a 'dependence on decontextualized, "product-based" analysis' (Marsh, 2008, p. 20), noting that patterns such as those on which the Kodály material is based are often derived from the generalisation of patterns seen in the play of children from a single context and may not be generalisable (for a discussion on this, see Marsh, 2008, pp. 10–11 and p. 305).

Second, a musical world founded on evolutionary developmental principles of moving from the simple to the complex assumes that the child is 'primitive' and by becoming immersed in tasks which are sequential and linear, moving from the simple to the complex, the child will come to understand music.

Third, is a concern that, as Marsh (2008) observes, in attempting to create '"universals" from decontextualized data, music educators and researchers into musical play traditions in the first half of the twentieth century created mythologized versions of these traditions which have direct implications for classroom practice' (p. 305). She argues for a 'playful' rather than 'playlike' pedagogy, 'one that takes account of the cultural nuances and realities of children's musical capabilities and preferences, providing cognitive, performative, creative, and kinesthetic challenge' (p. 318).

In her study of children's musical play she takes an ethnographic approach where she views the material 'within the subculture of the children in terms of the attributes that are important to them, rather than the qualities that adults perceive as "useful"' (p. 44). Her findings revealed that the children's musical play demonstrated a holistic grasp of skills, in contrast to the literature which suggests that children move through a linear sequence, from the simple to the complex. When playing they did not break the song into phrases but learned through observation and gradual participation into the song. The children were observed to engage in musical practices which the literature suggests are far beyond what is expected of them at the particular age group. Children were conscious of the level of difficulty involved in movement patterns, and worked with their peers to overcome these challenges, using the process described by Soviet psychologist Lev Vygotsky (1934/86) as 'scaffolding'. Marsh noticed that self-imposed challenge featured as a characteristic of their musical play and reflected that, by adhering to established models of musical development, teachers might inadvertently miss opportunities to challenge the young learner at a pace that matches their capacity and fail to acknowledge their musical play in all its variety and complexity, and recognise that it is neither universally applicable nor immutable.

> While it will always be the role of the teacher to extend children's musical horizons beyond their current repertoire, it can be done in conjunction with children's own preference and in line with their own proclivity for novelty. (p. 316)

In other words we need to take into account each song on its own merit, and to understand the sociocultural context of its emergence.

Conclusion

In this chapter we have explored the way in which a listenership paradigm has found its way into the classroom. We considered how the use of narrative applied as an organizing device to pieces identified as 'classics' lends itself well to ascribing meaning to the music as it unfolds over time. This reminds us of the concept of music as object discussed in Chapter 2. We considered music devised for pedagogical purposes, and our purpose in doing this was to explore ways in which children's musical worlds have been created from an adult perspective, and informed by a graded sequential approach to learning. We referred to Zoltan Kodály and Carl Orff as two composer–teachers who shared an interest in the idea of a 'universal' in music and childhood and contrasted their perspectives on play with one proposed by Kathy Marsh from her study of children's musical worlds.

Reflection tasks

Exploring sound

Consider the following scenarios:

Scenario 1: Teacher asks the children to collect from home as many pieces of junk as they can find. This can include cardboard boxes, empty cartons, home-made rattles and anything that can be used to make a sound. They will use them in class.

Scenario 2: Teacher gives each child a musical instrument and they are shown how to make a sound. On teacher's instructions, they begin to play their sound together in a group, and to respond to start and stop signals.

- Describe what might happen next in each scenario, identifying any similarities and differences.
- In your view, which of these events carries more value for the participants?

5

WAYS IN: ENTERING THE MUSICAL WORLDS OF CHILDREN

This chapter focuses on:

- Adult conceptions of musical childhood
- Presenting case studies of musical encounters initiated by children
- Identifying features of musical interactions in the playground
- Experiences with recorded music
- Modelling school-based teacher–learner roles and relationships

Introduction

This chapter begins by suggesting that approaches to music education tend to be under-pinned by conceptions of musical childhood held by adults. We assess the extent to which these conceptions have become embedded in our understanding of the musical worlds of children. We look at recent studies where researchers urge us not to neglect children's play in music education and to consider musical childhood on its own terms, where children are 'being and becoming in the world' and not preparing for adult-hood. We show how French sociologist Pierre Bourdieu's notion of habitus is applied by researchers in diverse cultural contexts, and draw on American psychologist Urie Bron-fenbrenner's ideas of ecological environment to look beyond the school environment to find ways in which the children draw on multiple and diverse sources when interacting musically with each other.

Conceptions of musical childhood held by adults

There are many instances of where a national ideal is promoted through music and intro-duced into the cultural life of a people. Sometimes this happens formally in a methodical way through the school system. At other times we see it passed down informally from generation to generation. Pierre Bourdieu's notion of habitus can help to explain how such practices can be passed down through generations. He used the term 'habitus' to describe the 'durably installed generative principle of regulated improvisations ... [which produces] practices' (Bourdieu and Passeron, 1990, p. 78). According to Bourdieu, this operates at an unconscious level and yet its impact is significant, as the following two studies illus-trate. Taken from Campbell and Wiggins (2012) collection of stories of children's musical cultures, the first is set in Uganda where song singing is repurposed as a means of socialis-ing young girls into adulthood and the second takes place in Singapore, introducing the notion of 'coiffuring' within a western classical music practice (see also Mackinlay, 2012).

Music and cultural socialisation into adulthood

The account provided by the Ugandan writer Nannyonga-Tamusuza (2012) focuses on cultural socialisation into womanhood and manhood. She argues that this process of socialisation begins when the child is born, and is ongoing and nuanced. 'Metaphoric, symbolic, and idiomatic language; girlhood lullabies; and musical tales and games are sites where gendered information, which would not otherwise be communicated in public, is "dressed up" to communicate a discourse that is otherwise only acceptable in private' (p. 128).

While music and play are part and parcel of children's life among the Baganda (the peoples of Buganda, 'formerly a powerful and dominant kingdom in central Uganda' (p. 115)), children's songs, musical tales and games have a role too in socialising rural

Baganda girls in womanhood. In the case of the girl, this socialisation focuses on her growth into a submissive wife and mother and music has a part to play in this: 'the songs sung to her and those that she sings' (p. 117). In this process of socialisation, the community is central and within this the family has a key part to play in introducing the child to the adult world. The adult roles of grandmother and paternal aunt are significant, with the grandmother tending to pass on the songs and folktales.

Coiffuring musical childhood

In an ethnographic study of the musical childhood of Clara, a fourth-generation Singaporean, Chee-Hoo Lum (Dairianathan and Lum, 2012) found a series of practices which were embedded within the environment – in this case the musical environment surrounding Clara – and interviews undertaken with the family involved in her upbringing confirmed to him that they support and promote these practices unquestioningly, and without considering an alternative. He describes how he became aware of parallels between the musical childhood he witnessed in Clara's home and memories of his own childhood. Although their childhoods are some 30 years apart, both were constructed from what he terms 'anglicized eurocentricity' (Dairianathan and Lum, 2012):

> We both grew up (and are still growing up) in an educational system driven by an economic model that favors English as the primary medium of instruction while our mother tongue is designated as a second language. We grew up with nursery rhymes such as 'London Bridge', 'Twinkle Twinkle Little Star', 'Old King Cole', and 'Humpty Dumpty' but also 'Liang Zhi Lau Hu' (Two Tigers) and 'Ke Ren Lai' (The Guest is Here). Our favorite Mandarin 'folk nursery songs' featured melodies taken from 'Frère Jacques' and were harmonized with I – IV – V chord progressions. (p. 338)

During his time with Clara and her family, he is constantly reminded of his own childhood and the role his parents played in cultivating a particular musical childhood, recognising the similarity between this and the part being played by Clara's parents.

> We were chauffeured around by our parents to piano lessons once or twice a week and kept under parental surveillance as we practiced our instruments at home … (p. 336)

In both cases, he explains that the family becomes complicit in perpetuating a particular musical world, imbuing it with value (or what Bourdieu terms capital) such that it acquires a position of privilege over all other possibilities. He draws on Bourdieu to suggest that the 'orchestration of habitus' entails the production of a commonsense world endowed with the objectivity secured by consensus on the meaning of practices and the world (Bourdieu, 1977, p. 80). Lum concludes that this 'commonsense world' has been orchestrated or carefully cultivated to give the impression that it has legitimacy in the culture, that it belongs there. He describes this as 'coiffuring' and notes that it permeates every field of the habitus – even the familial environment for a learner's education through music. It explains for him why Clara's parents invested in inculcating in her a disposition to music which could be evidenced by competent performance at ABRSM exams. 'Thousands of children continue to flow through their graded system, with parents thinking that this ABRSM validates, if not officialises, their children's musical development' (p. 344).

At the back of this lies both his and Clara's parents' interpretation of Confucian ethics, which he claims made them ideally placed to take up the notion of a musical childhood.

> Clara's musical childhood encompasses only what her parents have coiffured for her. (p. 340)

Constructed out of a notion that childhood is a phase of human development, it leads to a linear model of education, which is well served by graded examinations progressively increasing in challenge and skill level.

Teacher conceptions of musical childhood

Much has been written about conceptions of musical childhood held by teachers, particularly those working in primary school settings. In the main, the focus of research undertaken with and on this population tends to report on their perceived lack of confidence in teaching music to the children in the classroom setting. The 'music' being addressed is that presented in education systems as 'curriculum music'. The presentation of music as a specialist subject with expertise in performance and fluent in standard western notation pervades in these documents, as is evidenced by the emphasis on competence, and on the way in which music education is framed within notions of talent and musical ability. This comes with an assumption that teaching such 'music' is best left to others, to experts, to those with a particular set of skills necessary to bring about demonstrable improvement in children's abilities predominantly in performance. In our MaPS project (Stakelum and Baker, 2013) we set out to unearth some of these assumptions in order better to understand the conceptions held by primary teachers, and to explore their beliefs and attitudes about music as a school subject. The study was undertaken at a time of change in the music education landscape in England, following a review of the provision of music education (Department for Education, 2011a) and the National Plan for Music Education which followed (Department for Education, 2011c). Our concern was that the perpetuation of the status quo might continue to disempower those employed to teach children in the classroom context – the majority of the professionals within the primary school system – from engaging in music with their young learners. Following a review of the literature on our three main themes of interest, namely nature–nurture in beliefs about musical ability, the attributes associated with the musically able, and teacher beliefs on whether musical ability can be developed, we administered a questionnaire to a selection of schools in the south-east of England (see further details in Stakelum and Baker, 2013). Our findings confirmed that those whose knowledge base maped onto that presented in the curriculum document believed that music was teachable. This is hardly surprising as we might expect that, following Bourdieu, they have a shared cultural capital and so are likely to be at home with the selection and organisation of music as a school subject, and can replicate or reproduce the dominant culture with ease. What was more troubling to us was the finding of those whose experiences of music did not map onto music as defined in the curriculum. Here the respondents reported that they did not think that music was teachable. This was confirmed further in the response to our question about markers of 'musicality' in themselves and in their peers. Those who self-identified as non-musical did so because they did not play a musical instrument. While they agreed that family background and environment had a bearing on conceptions of musicality, they distinguished between formative experiences that were formal and those that took place in formal contexts. For example, where singing was cited as an activity, it denoted for them an activity outside the formal setting of the school and in social situations, like church choirs and family gatherings. In contrast, when giving reasons to support their descriptions of themselves or their peers as 'musical', they almost exclusively mentioned formal instrumental tuition as the deciding factor. Crucially, the way in which they value one set of practices over another is likely to have a bearing on their own relationship with music education and in how they see their role in contributing to, and informing, the musical childhoods of those with whom they come in contact in the formal school setting.

Implications for practice

Let's look again at the vignette in Chapter 1. It describes a choir rehearsal in a primary school with the teacher, Fiona, putting the finishing touches to a piece of choral music in advance of a public performance. Fiona was brought up in a musical world of classical music and enjoyed performing, as evidenced by her progress through grades and her successful entry to music at higher education. Clearly her intention was to share this love of music with the learners in her care: indeed this was one of the factors motivating her to become a teacher. In addition to passing on her love of music, she wants to provide them with a passport to a better world, to open up opportunities for them to extend their options. In effect she wants to replace their habitus with hers. What we don't know from the study is the long-term impact of her intervention on these young learners – this was not the focus of the study at the time. It is interesting to reflect on how their perceptions of these formative experiences might fit with Lum's reflective account of 'coiffuring'.

To summarise, we have seen the mores and customs valued by the community with the Ugandan village being passed on from one generation to the next through music and song. We have seen also how a nation's musical culture could be constructed from folksongs and be presented as a child's birthright. While these scenarios are not in any way comprehensive they remind us that just as children do not live in a vacuum, neither are their musical childhoods impervious to the environment around them. When considering the implications of this for music education, we are reminded of Blacking's observation that 'the unit is not the individual organism but the population-in-environment' (Blacking, 1987, p. 79). Children's musical development must also be seen to happen not in isolation but within some sociocultural context.

Bronfenbrenner (1979) likened this to an ecological environment, and imagined it as a range of interconnected networks. Conceived topographically, it is a nested arrangement of concentric structures, each one contained within the next.

> At the innermost level is the immediate setting containing the developing person…The next … requires looking beyond single settings to the relations between them… The third level is one with which the developing person might not be directly connected. (p. 3)

He emphasises the importance of each setting in shaping the child's development, and even where the child is not directly present there is a connection between each of the surroundings which influences the growth and development of the child. It is this complex network of interconnections that lies at the heart of the learning environment (see Bronfenbrenner, 1979, pp. 21f for his expansion on this). Bronfenbrenner's extended conception of the environment is considerably broader and more differentiated than that found in a school environment influenced by psychology in general and developmental psychology in particular. In the next section we look beyond what we know about music education from research undertaken within a schooling environment towards a recognition that understanding children's interactions with environments outside school is an important part of understanding their musical worlds.

Child-initiated musical interactions

Patricia Shehan-Campbell (2010) recognises that children are who they are as a result of growing up within families, neighbourhoods and a variety of communities, each one with its own particular information to impart. She suggests that the music of the family is linked to the larger cultural community that generates what she terms 'the sonic surrounds of [their] musical sensibilities' (Campbell, 2011, p. 64). Pointing to the influence of musical enculturation and socialisation, she notes that, although the two are related, they differ in respect of the level of engagement. Whereas enculturation comes about through osmosis, by absorbing everything around them, socialisation involves direct engagement: '[s]ocialization requires members of a social group (parents and grandparents, for example) to interact with children in order to inculcate the beliefs and values of that social group' (p. 66).

Like Campbell (2010), Marsh (2011) suggests that children's interactions with the world around them influence their musical play and meaning-making. By observing children at play, she notes that we can gain access to their musical worlds and recognise that children are expert teachers within their own milieu (p. 57).

In her research on musical play in the playground, Marsh found that the children drew on cultural influences from multiple sources that inform their world. These cultural influences extend across the proximal, include parents, siblings and other relatives, to more distant environments, contributing to the development of new and emerging musical worlds. She notes the fluid nature of this process and the role of technologies in expanding the cultural influences.

Increasingly, these new technologies create access to a continually expanding range of cultural artefacts and practices, which influence and interact with localized versions to produce 'new cultural hybrids' in a process termed transculturation (Lull, 2000). (Marsh, 2011, p. 43)

Marsh and Young (2006) note that much of what is known about musical play comes from research into adult-initiated events, predominantly from within the industrialised, high-income world. Their starting point for understanding the phenomenon of musical play is to define it as 'the activities that children initiate of their own accord and in which they may choose to participate with others voluntarily' (p. 289). They outline musical play as multimodal, involving kinaesthetic, visual and aural activities. It is spontaneous, and even when based on recognisable styles it retains an improvisational and unplanned character. It is a form of social interaction, promoting collaboration and cohesion within friendship groups (Marsh, 1995). It involves rules of turn-taking and hierarchical structures of social importance, reinforcing Blacking's (1967) observation about reflecting and endorsing enculturated behaviours and social patterns from the wider sociocultural environment.

Marsh undertook an extensive investigation of musical play, spanning the years between 1990 and 2004 and several continents (Australia, the United States, England, Norway and Korea). As part of her study, she explored the way in which, when left to themselves, children in the playground engaged with music and with each other. What she found was an oral tradition, where the children sounded out the various permutations of their song, selecting those which met with their approval, rejecting others, and through multiple performances arriving at a final, agreed version through a method in which composition and improvisation were interlinked.

She observed that the process of composition was linked with performance of the singing games, and furthermore that the process was not a solitary one but co-constructed, involving groups of children. This was very much a collaborative approach: 'part of the process of thinking out and sounding out that characterises generative practices in musical play in this context' (Marsh, 2008, p. 202).

Much of this collaborative work took place within a period of minutes, during which she observed a number of different developmental modes set out by Swanwick and Tillman's (1986) model of children's composition.

[I]nherent in the Swanwick and Tillman model is the assumption that these processes are developmental and that this development is age-related to some extent... Yet in the compositional sequence documented above, the children would appear to be collaboratively working through a number of different developmental modes within a period of several minutes. The first recitation of the text exhibits features of the Speculative mode, followed by a period in which they are developing Manipulative control of movement materials, after which successive performances appear to be related to first Vernacular and then Idiomatic modes. (pp. 206–7)

In refuting the linear developmental model of Swanwick and Tillman 1986, Marsh suggests that compositional processes vary according to the context within which they are enacted and that the importance of group interaction is recognised (see Marsh 2008, p. 206f). This is significant not least because it questions the notion that children's musical development can be tracked linearly, and moves in stages, mirroring in musical terms Piaget's claim that children's development moves incrementally from stage to stage. It differs too from the context within which Paynter and Aston (1970) set Alan's solitary play-like movements. It also asks us to consider collaborative musicking in the playground context as a valid learning experience. There are lessons for teachers here too, and implications for music education. Marsh suggests that we start with where the children are, rather than imposing a set of directed tasks. 'Just as playground culture is permeable, so the culture of the classroom can draw on divergent sources for musical and pedagogical enrichment' (Marsh, 2011, p. 58).

Working within a Ghanaian context, Mary Dzansi (2004) conducted research on three schools and a neighbourhood community over a four-month period. Her participants were aged between 6 and 15, and based in city and village sites. She spent a month in each school and observed playground activity, recording and carrying out unstructured interviews with the children and subsequently with parents. She found that, in the process of performing singing games, those who do not know stand at the periphery to observe those who know. Leadership roles were shared and everyone took turns to take on the role of leaders. The children were their own teachers. They could coordinate two or more activities – singing, clapping and dancing – and when asked, those participating noted that they picked it up, they did not consciously practice the actions separately but holistically developed their mastery of whichever actions were required. Learning by doing was a feature of this pedagogy. She contrasts this with formal classroom pedagogy and points out that the joy, the laughter and the seriousness with which they performed their music activities might be transferred to the classroom. It would work if teachers could reimagine their role as adult expert to move away from drill and rote learning of activities in isolation, call on the young learners to demonstrate and involve everyone in playful learning.

We find further compelling evidence that children are not impervious to the world around them in Ingeborg Vestad's (2014) exploration of children's everyday uses of recorded music. Her study was set in the Norwegian kindergarten context where she devised a way of capturing children's engagement with music during their `free play' activities. In each of the two settings, she sat with a camcorder on her lap and, when someone (adult or child/ren) played a CD or other recorded music, she used the camcorder to record the way in which the children responded to what they heard. She complemented this with her own field notes and with interviews conducted with adults in the settings and with the children. There were nine children who engaged particularly strongly and a second phase of her study included them in their family settings. She loaned a camcorder to each of the nine families and requested that they record for a week the engagement of their child with recorded music. Following this, she held an interview with each family. In making sense of the data, she identifies two narratives about music. The first is that music is something that everyone can do, an idea based on the fact that musical skills are naturally evolving and available to all. A second narrative counters this, and it is that 'only the talented can'. This was found to be held by parents who had identified the child in the family who was 'the musical one'. This tendency to categorise musical and non-musical extends beyond the study and resonates with perceptions held more widely. We see it also in the study carried out in Sweden by Pernilla Lagerlöf and Cecilia Wellerstedt (2019), who used 'frames' to make sense of video observation and interactions between and among six children, aged 3–5 years – Asa, Moa, Tea, Ida, Tom and Per – in a preschool setting when left to their own devices. They reported on four frames in all, and in each one their concern was first to explore how these children negotiated the play frame in the studied activity and from there to examine how they actualised their previous experience of a musical performance.

In their analysis, the researchers traced the children's musical play to their interpretative reproduction of a song contest which was known to them from a popular TV show. A number of strategies could be observed, from initial resistance to the roles ascribed to them, to finding ways to get their way in a discussion, and to taking ownership of the performance. The findings reveal that there is a level of complexity around the way in which musical play occurs. Not only did the children struggle to get the courage to sing but also had difficulty in knowing what song to sing. What was interesting too was that the children themselves demonstrated some of the norms and beliefs about music as something that requires a certain talent or disposition. 'The analysis ... sheds light on preschool as an arena where children act against the backdrop of experienced performances of professional artists, perfectly edited sound, juries that judge performances in public' (p. 95). It underpins too the message these young children pick up from the media, that 'only the talented are supposed to sing or else the crowd may laugh or the jury may send you home' (p. 95), and that they too are put in the position of judges through social media (p. 95). The researchers conclude that there is a role for the teacher in these preschool settings which look on the surface like zones of free play. 'Since digitalised resources and media are a part of young children's lives, they need help from adults to sort out their experiences and to afford them complementary experiences that the child can relate to' (p. 96).

Tina Kullenberg's (2014) study captures the extent to which the relationship between teacher and learner has become embedded as one of master–apprentice in the interactions of four children, aged 9 and 10, who were teaching each other to sing songs, specifically chosen from Swedish culture and based on traditional western tonality. She wanted to learn about how children value and organise musical knowledge 'in action' outside a school situation and without a guiding adult in their immediate vicinity. She did this by setting up teaching activities as 'social encounters in cultural practices' (p. 8).

The encounters take place between an instructor (or instructors) and an apprentice (or apprentices) and where the participants involved share an agreed purpose: to deal with the apprentice's specific learning outcome. That means an *intended* and contracted learning outcome, with the instructor as the pedagogical leader. (p. 8; italics in original)

The children were recruited with help from a music teacher in a primary school. Of those who volunteered the researcher selected four who seemed to get on with each other: Michael, Amy, Paul and Diana. Interviews with pairs were conducted. In each pair, one partner – the expert – knew the song to be taught and was assigned to the role of `teacher'. The other did not know the song and was willing to learn, and took the role of the pupil.

The children taught each other songs in dyads (two by two) as a pre-given task, without the presence of an adult in the ongoing activity (p. 8). Five sessions in all were videoed. The sessions took place in the researcher's home with a video camera positioned on a bookcase in a fixed position, turned on by the researcher before leaving the room. The children would decide when they felt the task was completed. All of the teaching episodes were of 30–40 minutes' duration. Analysis of the five sessions showed that they drew on a number of ritual conventions: counting the singer in, thereby bringing some order to the event; teacher-initiated critical evaluation of the singing, mainly around correcting, approval and criticism from the teacher; and dialogue about the song performance.

There were gestures too which the 'teacher' inhabited – pointing to and nodding at certain features. The 'pupil' used facial expressions to convey emotions – smiling as they tried to bring up challenging learning moments or to express their sense of achievement. All of these communicative and pedagogical aspects of the interaction demonstrate the dialogicality involved in teaching and learning, and the extent to which they are picked up by children on their own, outside the formal classroom setting.

Kullenberg's point is that sense-making in teaching and learning does not occur in a vacuum (p. 196); it relies on building trust through emotive gestures. '[D]ecisive emotions are at stake in the evaluative pedagogical dialogues: [illustrating] the intricate relation between emotional trust and interpersonal teaching (and learning)' (p. 198). She provides a fascinating insight into the children's engagement with each other during this teaching and learning process, and points to double dialogicality in their practice. A dialogical approach can be seen in the way the children were conversing and communicating about the song and how to perform it, and at the same time as this, they were acting out an underlying social rule very strictly, "always respecting the teacher's right to take verbal initiatives, to correct mistakes and to judge the singing efforts" (p. 201). She explains how their role play as teacher and learner operates at a double dialogical level when 'the children's attention was also directed to the consistent reproduction of formalised education-specific social structures' (p. 204) and brings to mind Bernstein's (2000) notion of pedagogic discourse: 'those who reproduce legitimate knowledge *institutionalize the thinkable*, whilst those who *produce* legitimate knowledge *institutionalize the unthinkable*' (2014, p. 204; italics in original).

[T]he children who enacted the pupil role expected the 'teachers' to give orders, request actions, explain things, ask and make assessments when they wanted pupils to implement ideas and pedagogical training. (pp. 96–7)

Not only do the dialogues take place at a local, situated and interpersonal level but also with sociohistorical (and sociocultural) praxis. 'Accordingly, the children not only orient to each other's signing and singing acts in their pedagogical practice, but also to knowledge, conventions and norms of music-life in society and formalised, institutional pedagogy from school-life' (p. 199). All four had a shared understanding of what ii means to participate in (musical) schooling. They could reproduce the rules of the game, and the routines of teaching, and modelled their activities on what they experienced in school.

In her study on Greek Cypriot children's musical identities, Avra Pieridou Skoutella (2019) set out to give voice to their musical practices. Her experience as a teacher led her to observe that 'the music lesson is subject-focused, state controlled and target driven, … and understood from a top-down approach' (p. 6). Moreover, she found that 'music as a curriculum subject has been irrelevant and almost entirely disconnected from children's and teachers' musical abilities, interests, musical worlds and identities' (p. 6).

She took an ethnographic and ethnomusicological approach to finding out what meanings these children made of the music in their lives, and how these played out in different contexts, as they move, live and act in and through different geographical, musical and social contexts (p. 8). She was influenced by Campbell's (2010) work on showing how children's cultures and practices are anchored to adults' cultural values and practices and are thus socially, politically, culturally, historically and economically contextualised by the adult world. She conducted her fieldwork in a rural site of several villages and an urban site, and interviewed participants in each site were children between 9 and 11. She observed lessons, and musical practices outside school and lots of other things.

Pieridou Skoutella found that the urban children were displaying signs of discriminating between low and high forms of musical enculturation, dissociating themselves from Cypriot cultural practices in favour of westernised musical identities. This tended to result in a narrower range of musical experiences than those children at the rural site in two significant ways. The first was that the children did not participate in high forms of culture unless they were considered to be sufficiently talented or nurtured through formal education. This attitude filtered through from school, which supported instrumental tuition. The second was that there was a predominance of consumption of music. In other words they listened to music and were heavily influenced by the media and the music industry. She notes that the children's musical practices were disconnected from those of adults in this regard. Children in the rural setting had a wider range of music experiences, including local social activities involving adults and with Cypriot music and dance where they participate among themselves and others. She found their relationship with classical music to be interesting. It was categorised as old and belonging to a decontextualised ahistorical past and was seen as high-status musical culture. For those who had been labelled 'talented' it was important to show that they stood out from their peers and they did this by discussing aspects of their instrumental lessons or a subject related to classical music which was known only to those who were insiders in this musical world. 'They were proud to show that they were party to a musical tradition that is considered difficult to learn and to understand, and a tradition that belongs only to the few who have the potential and the means to learn it' (p. 189).

'Speaking for ourselves': listening to the sounds of those who do not sing

The final section of this chapter takes its title from Michael Bakan's (2018) set of conversations with 10 people. All of the participants had two things in common: a life in which music figures prominently and an autism spectrum diagnosis (p. xxi). His research was motivated by an aim to give voice to this population so that they could speak for themselves rather than have others speak for them, a recognition that the term 'autism', what the phrase 'autism spectrum' means, and how to respond to the challenges and opportunities of neurodiversity, are not fixed or static but constantly in flux, and a belief that we can 'make up' a better world than the one we have now: 'more inclusive, more humane, and more compassionate; a world in which our seemingly unassailable drive to classify and categorise one another directs us towards knowledge rather than fear, acceptance rather than exclusion, and conversation rather than objectification' (p. 15).

These conversations grew from collaborative projects called Music-Play-Project (2005–2009) and a neurodiverse music group called the Artism Ensemble (2011–2013), and led him to raise with his collaborators key topics ranging from musical stimming, alternative modes of musicking, autism acceptance and the vagaries of normalcy (p. 3). Through his account of one such conversation, we see how Zena, aged 10, struggled with other people's efforts to get her to join in with the musical activities. It was through her mother (Suzanne in the story) that the author was made aware of this: 'She wants to be able to listen and respond to the music "in her own way", explained the mother, even if that means just flapping her hands and twisting her fingers and pacing round the room' (p. 24). Zena presented two contrasting modes of participation in the music experiences. One was through stimming and the other was playing on the E-WoMP instruments with the other ensemble members, and she moved between the two of these. As the leader came to realise, she engaged in each one, preferring one to the other at various times: neither one was superior to the other and the group came to appreciate this. In the conversation with Zena, it emerged that what appeared to the group as non-participation was in fact a deep concentration as she imagined characters in her head playing the instruments and it seemed unnecessary for her to play. As she became more comfortable in the group she felt less pressurised to play and began to realise that she could express herself in any way of her choosing. For her that moment was when the characters in her head merged and became her. She had reconfigured the ensemble by imagining the Band of Brothers performing, and concentrating on the sound each of the instruments played.

Conclusion

We have seen that the beliefs held by adults cast a long shadow and influence the shaping of discourses on musical childhoods. We noted too a growing awareness of the importance of including children's perspectives, and of exploring the reciprocal relationship between the child and the environment more broadly. Observing child-initiated musical interactions can teach us much about music education and play pedagogy, revealing new insights which invite us to review some commonly held assumptions about musical childhood.

Reflection tasks

Chartwell Dutiro was born in Zimbabwe and his travels with mbira music took him from his home village to playing in pubs, halls and community centres around the cosmopolitan city of Harare with the Zimbabwean band Thomas Mapfumo & the Blacks Unlimited, where he mixed mbira with guitar, lead guitar, bass and drumkit. From there he travelled further afield internationally to venues such as London's Royal Festival Hall, Southbank, Royal Albert Hall and the Globe theatre, and to New York. He settled in Devon and used mbira as an education tool to connect with people and build bridges between cultures. In an interview with me, he shared his insights into the concept of 'children's musical worlds' and identified some of the challenges he found when teaching in education systems such as that in England with a culture of teaching and learning built around music as a specialist subject.

> In Africa, music is central. We sing when we are sad, we sing when we are happy, we sing when we celebrate. You know, I've met people who have said 'I was just thrown out of the school choir and I never sing'. What is that about? [A]ll about taking people down.
>
> The mbira is a sacred traditional instrument of Zimbabwe. When we play the music it has got a purpose and the purpose of the mbira is to connect the people with the spirit of their ancestors… We talk about spirit in different contexts but when I say 'connect with the spirit of your ancestors' people aren't comfortable with that. What is that about? And yet we have [TV] programmes like *Who Do You Think You Are*? And it is exactly that is the model that African people already have… The music is passed down from generation to generation… This is my DNA – this is my grandfather, this is my father, my grandmother.
>
> You go into a place, an educational place, and there are tables, chairs and computers: 'Oh, we use this. This room is for computers but we thought we should play here, and do your lecture here.' And I'm thinking 'I need students to be sitting around me'.

Consider these insights in light of your relationship with music and draw on Campbell's concept of 'the sonic surrounds of your musical sensibilities' to explore how music education might connect you with the music of your family, community and extended musical worlds.

6

MUSIC CREATED WITH CHILDREN

This chapter focuses on:

- Applying a social pedagogy to music with care experienced children and carers
- Creating space for a pedagogy of play with very young children
- Extending the boundaries of music through listening
- Learning a musical instrument as a means towards engaging with orchestral performance practice

Introduction

This chapter uses a range of music initiatives chosen from small-scale community pro-grammes and larger-scale public funded ones to shed light on settings which are con-ceived as educational in somewhat unconventional ways. Though based in England, the projects will be broad in scope and relevance to a wider audience. There are four in all, and each one is presented as a paradigm or world view. The first of these is designed to 'support the musical, personal, emotional and communication development of particu-lar focus groups of early years children (looked after, adopted children and children on the edge of care), [and...] helps to build and nurture relationships between these children and their birth families, foster carers, adoptive parents and peers or siblings' (inspire-music, n.d.). Musicians, local authority foster care support staff and community foster care staff work together using principles of social pedagogy which ensure that the work is enacted in the best interests of potentially vulnerable and young participants. The sec-ond initiative described in this chapter is Magic Adventure, a project designed by expe-rienced early childhood music specialist/artist-educators in partnership with the young children in their practice and with babies and toddlers in mind. It combines methods of playfulness and complicité drawn from art forms not commonly associated with early childhood. These include contemporary clowning, physical theatre, jazz improvisation and music therapy, and complement the child-led interaction with the physical land-scape, combining exploratory play with interactive playfulness co-created between chil-dren, adults and the world (Magic Adventure, 2013). In the third initiative, the focus is on extending the horizons of children and young people through engaging with sounds. Listening is presented as experiential, individual, shared and collective, as a stimulus to other activities, and an invitation to inhabit multiple modes of engaging in and with the world (Minute of Listening, 2022). The fourth initiative is built on principles of presenta-tional performance and is called In Harmony. It is described on its website as 'a national programme that aims to inspire and transform the lives of children in deprived commu-nities, using the power and disciplines of ensemble music-making' (Arts Council, n.d.).

Each of the four initiatives is described in terms of underlying rationale, aims and objectives. An analysis of documents in the public domain forms an evidence base for much of this, including the Paul Hamlyn Foundation-funded website inspire-music. The website is very much a living space, with new projects added continually to present examples of music education in England as it happens in a diverse range of settings, contexts and configurations. The chapter ends with a consideration of the importance of place in children's musical worlds outlined in the four paradigms and how each one contributes to our understanding of music education.

Social pedagogy paradigm

Loud and Clear is a programme focused on music in early childhood (0–5). First estab-lished in 2009, the programme was funded through the national singing programme Sing

Up to work alongside partners with primary-aged children in challenging circumstances, including looked after children. Funded by Youth Music it began as a pilot project linking early years and family learning teams in two local authorities, Gateshead and Newcastle, and with a particular concern for supporting foster carers and adoption partners. Following from this, in 2011 partners from local authorities in the North East of England, Sage Gateshead and local councils found a way to develop the project to target children in the 0–5 year age group and were awarded funding from Youth Music to do this over 3 years.

The programme takes its name from reassigning the initials LAC (looked after children) to convey the point that care experienced young people and children have voices that need to be heard (loud and clear) rather than be marginalized, which up until that point, particularly in terms of music, arguably has been the case. While the term 'looked after children' has now been replaced by 'care experienced children', the brand LAC has continued to be used to refer to the programme of making music with very young children (0–5) who are care experienced or looked after children, and their carers.

As a programme which values the carer–cared for relationship, and recognises that 'becoming human' takes place via relationships with other human beings in small and large social groups and institutions, it aligns itself with principles of social pedagogy (see Cameron et al., 2021, p. 5). It moves away from the task-based and procedural to the relational and reflective, from the functional to the educative (2021, p. 10). Social pedagogues do not direct those in the group but work alongside them. They work from a starting point of respect for the whole person, individuals as physical beings and social beings, recognising that they too are beings with thoughts and feelings. What this means is that they have no pre-ordained or pre-envisioned goal in mind. Nor do they compartmentalise the work they do into tasks targeted at one particular cognitive domain but consider the holistic nature of being and becoming. For the partners working on the programme this has particular resonance as the carers learn alongside the musicians and develop a shared understanding of the purpose of the workshops, and learn a common language built on shared values.

The Loud and Clear sessions on music offered foster carers an opportunity to take part in music workshops, and to consider ways in which music might be used to connect them with the young children in their care, to connect the care experienced child with their birth family and to remind them of their foster carer family when they moved on. For example, in the Early Years toolkit session the workshop leaders would explore with the participating foster carers items in their homes that they could use to make music with the children they look after. Songs they had sung in the workshops together were compiled into a songbag - something that the young children could take with them when they moved to their foster carer, back to their birth family or to adoption. For adoptive parents too, this served an important purpose as it provided them with stories of the adoption process which they could share with parents in mainstream music groups or parent–baby groups where conversations take place about birth stories and feeding stories. Having the songbags allows them to take part and to feel included.

A collaborative approach between all the agencies involved within the local authorities was key to the success of the programme. Its success hinged on those local authority teams seeing the value of it and promoting it to families with whom they worked, with each partner convinced of its value in making a difference to the lives and potential of those for whom it was devised.

The practitioners are trained in skills which prepare them for the sensitive nature of relationships at the heart of this programme, and their knowledge of how to use music as a tool to build attachments between the children and their peers or siblings, between families, adoptive parents and foster care families. Training built in for foster carers is mapped to the child development workforce training required of them. The children learn social skills, routines and strategies to support them in transitioning from care to adoptive families, and from care to birth families. They learn too the importance of playful relationships with others and the musical activities they encounter are built on communication, cooperation and trust.

The songbags and songbooks developed for the children in partnership with the foster carers help to bridge the emotional distance the young children travel when moving from one home to another. The songbags contain finger puppets, CDs and accessible percussion instruments (easy to use and capable of producing sounds through shaking, scraping and tapping), all of which were given to the parents and foster parents at the end of the project. These would form a standalone resource which could be used to continue the music making with the children at home, thus providing further continuity. In addition, a songbook was compiled for the foster families.

The sessions took place weekly and were 90 minutes long, to include 60 minutes of music making and time for discussion and informal conversation between project partners and participating adults. The adults reported increased levels of confidence in the children and there was qualitative anecdotal evidence of positive benefits for the children. Musicians noted in their journals that foster carers who attended the weekly music-making sessions found that they could help develop musical skills such as pulse and rhythm awareness, and listening skills including awareness of pitch, timbre/tone, dynamics/volume, beat/pulse and tempo/speed. Alongside this, vocal skills such as singing, playing with vocal sound and speech confidence were improved. And there was attention to basic pre-instrumental and simple songwriting skills.

The multi-agency model of intervention provided by Loud and Clear was found to be successful and even after the initial years of its implementation, there was some evidence that music making was helping to bridge the transition between foster care and 'forever family', most notably through the case study of 'George' provided in the evaluation report undertaken by Anderson et al. (Anderson, J., Little, J. and Mooney, E. (nd), pp. 26–7). George was involved in the project in the first year as a looked after child attending with his foster carer and in the second year with his new family. This continuity provided valuable insights to the team about the tangible benefits of the project.

There were lessons learned by the musicians too, and they reported a deeper and extended understanding of the issues faced by this population and increased sensitivity to individual needs of children, parents and carers within music sessions. In the first two years of the project, they reported 'feeling more attuned to the groups within this project as a direct result of this project's emphasis on attachment and the time factored in to allow for conversation and shared reflection' (p. 31). The use of reflection as a device for developing their own expertise was also seen as a benefit.

Playful place paradigm

Magic Adventure is 'a luminous, musical, interactive spectacular for babies and toddlers' (Magic Adventure, 2013). Created in 2001, it is underpinned by a strong pedagogical underpinning and rationale and forms part of Magic Acorns, an organisation which defines itself as encountering the world with children, learning what children can do from children, and what art can do by listening to children.

> We create aesthetic work, which is made for – and with – children under five.
>
> - We forge connections and grow communities through the creation of inclusive, enriching and compassionate spaces, for children, parents, artists and educators.
> - We foster collaboration between arts and cultural organisations, artists and educators.
> - We support participation, developing skills through training, experimentation, exploration and reflection.
> - We keep research at the heart of practice and develop deep thinking through theoretical approaches. (Magic Acorns, 2020)

The Magic Adventure cast are highly skilled in co-creating with children and working in many modes – movement, gesture, facial expression, voice play, sound play, object play and funniness.

As an initiative it maps onto the principles of the Early Years Foundation Stage, which sets the standards of learning, development and care of children from birth to 5. We have seen in Chapter 1 how this foundation stage emphasises playing and exploring, active learning, and creating and thinking differently, and sets out seven interconnected areas of learning and development, encouraging providers to engage with innovative responses to meeting these expectations.

In the case of Magic Adventure, each performance or 'happening' is interactive and takes place over 80 minutes or so in a large installation made of white fabric and coloured lights, with space for about 20 participants, to include adults and children. The cast members set up a residency over several days, working closely with practitioners in local nursery settings, children's centres and preschools to ensure that the goals of the programme are understood. These goals are listed on the website as follows:

> to:
>
> Create (and inspire others to create) an inspirational and immersive environment for very young children and their parents, carers and educators;

Promote and showcase improvisational techniques as a pedagogical tool for supporting child-led exploration, discovery, and communication; and

Develop understanding of young children's multimodal expression – which assimilates music, movement, funniness, voice-play, facial expression and a variety or material objects.

During the happening, the cast use voice-play, singing and playful interaction to communicate. Adults take their lead from the child in exploring and discovering the three-dimensional aural space, following their musical choices and individual lines of enquiry, all the time being alongside as they respond and engage with the children. This non-directive approach is a central feature of the ethos of Magic Adventure and arguably one of the challenges facing adults who are in positions of caring and responsibility for children. In light of this, the cast work with the adults to support them as they in turn support the children, and learn how to encourage playfulness in themselves and in their children. Because the cast are skilled musicians they are at home with improvising and performing, and can respond to musical stimuli provided by the children, and to the impulses emerging from the group. For educators and artists in the community who are less experienced in creative improvisatory work, professional development is offered. By the time the happening begins, all adults are in tune with the structure and shape of what is to come, and understand the nature and purpose of each section. For example, during open-ended, explorative sections in the session, large 'pallets' containing high-quality musical instruments are placed around the environment. A soundscape track is played during these explorations, which is in the same pentatonic scale as used by the tuned instruments. Short set pieces happen periodically throughout the show – songs, light shows – which introduce new elements or provoke new interactions.

New horizons paradigm

In 2008, Contemporary Music Network, Society for the Promotion of New Music, British Music Information Centre and The Sonic Arts Network, four groups sharing an interest in new music, merged to form Sound and Music, a national portfolio organisation with responsibility for developing innovative ways of engaging with the public. One of the initiatives of Sound and Music is Minute of Listening, which aims to create a world where children and young people are inspired and enabled to listen creatively every day through a series of curated pieces of music and soundscapes (Minute of Listening, 2022). It is designed for use in school and the resources are freely available (since 2021) for use in home and school education settings. There is no prescriptive approach but an awareness of a variety of starting points and this is reflected in the resource materials, the worksheets compiled for classroom practice and the breadth of listening examples provided.

This model of listening has potential to be transformative as a pedagogical approach. There is potential for listeners to move away from what Michael Gallagher et al. (2017) label 'a narrow understanding of listening as the conscious reception and comprehension of symbolic meanings encoded in spoken language' (p. 1246) towards 'a pedagogy for expanded listening' (p. 1247). There is potential to extend the minute of listening to a listening walk, a practice developed in acoustic ecology and experimental music, and which involves walking through an environment paying close attention to whatever sounds are encountered. 'Meaning is as much something we bring to sound as something sound brings to us' (p. 1251). In their project they included reflections of early years practitioners on a listening walk offered as professional development opportunity. As a pedagogy they suggest that 'the listening walk invites listeners to listen to their own listening' (p. 1248). Gallagher et al. note that although listening is listed as an early learning goal (Department for Education, 2014), it tends to be linked with a developmental trajectory in listening which is mapped onto communication and language skills rather than musical or sonic awareness. Their concern is that this sets in place a notion of the ideal child who 'territorialises sound into language, and sonic responsiveness into auditory comprehension' (p. 1249), a notion they are keen to dispel.

Presentational performance paradigm

Inspired by the work of El Sistema in Venezuela, in Harmony is founded on a principle of learning music together as a team, where children learn an instrument and play in ensemble together. There are six In Harmony programmes in all, and each one differs in terms of the length of time they have been established, their aims, the number of participating primary schools, their organizational and management structures, their access to professional orchestral musicians, their geographical location, the number and type of extracurricular activities, the instruments on offer, the content of the programmes, the extent of partnership networks and the ease of collecting progression data (Hallam and Burns, 2017). Since its launch in 2008 with funding from the Department for Children, Families and Schools for three pilots over two years, it has grown from being a social programme to one that aspires to be inspirational, raising the expectations and life chances of children through a high-quality music education (Hallam and Burns, 2017).

National Foundation for Educational Research (NFER)/Arts Council England (ACE) have defined the core principles as:

- a focus on areas of deprivation and low engagement;
- a demand-led, committed whole school approach;
- immersive and intensive activity;
- alignment with music education hubs/integration within music education hubs;
- professional musicians, ensembles and orchestras working with schools;

- high profile performance opportunities;
- continuity and progression for children;
- access to instruments;
- the sharing of expertise and resources. (Hallam and Burns, 2017, p. 5)

Over time, the core principles of In Harmony have evolved to reflect how the six programmes operate in their different settings. Following a musical progression report (Hallam and Burns, 2017), and to test the findings, the six In Harmony programmes undertook action research, including new activities and support for children in significantly disadvantaged communities wanting to continue their musical learning (Hallam and Burns, 2018). The most effective programmes were underpinned by a peer support and mentoring approach, where the older learners model behaviours and practices for the younger learners. Ensembles that span a wide range of year groups can be effective, fostering collaborative and respectful learning. Some programmes provided opportunities for team teaching with classroom practitioners and visiting specialist musicians working together. Over time the programme has become embedded in the life of schools in many of the sites visited, integrated into the day and across the various stages of the school curriculum. The participants reported that for them the camaraderie and bonding among their peers was a positive experience, though there were some concerns that they might be singled out by non-ensemble members. The orchestra becomes a vehicle for learning more than music as the transferability of learning spills over to other areas of their lives such as developing confidence, courage and other soft skills in themselves. More broadly, they learn how performing can impact on their community, and being part of an orchestra can endow their community with pride. The teaching team supports them and encourages them to take the music to the community, including residential homes, cinema, shops and the wider world. The teachers took it as a professional development opportunity with the learning process as relevant to the teachers as well as to the learners. In these instances it became a whole – school project. The transition from primary to secondary school was noted as an anxious period in young people's lives and the research found that communication with the secondary school was vital in terms of smoothing the move from primary school. In some cases the children did not reveal to the teachers in their new school that they had had the In Harmony experience in their primary school. One way of mitigating this was to create a music profile of each young musician so that this could be passed on to the new school.

We can see that each of the six programmes started out with the same general purpose: not simply to perform but to develop resilience, esteem, confidence and life skills. We can see too that the communicative power of music is explored through interaction with peers and with adults. The success rested greatly on the sensitivity of the facilitators to the children, and in some cases building in continuing professional development opportunities for the practitioners ensured that there would be a legacy beyond the product or length of each individual project. The multi-agency factor was found to be key. Where the child's voice was included, it was interesting to see how they had a level of awareness of the need for negotiating, for respecting the views of others, and the courage and motivation to voice their preferences.

Conclusion

Each of the initiatives presented above originated from a belief held by the project leaders in the importance of music in the lives of children and young people. The way in which this works in practice differs and gives each one its distinctive characteristic. The Loud and Clear programme is based on principles of social pedagogy where music is a means by which the child is considered not as an object of learning but in a holistic sense, with due regard for the nurturing of relationships with adults who are significant in their lives. Music practitioners work alongside the children and care workers, choosing activities to ensure that all the participants can engage fully in the experiences, and that memories created will sustain them as they move from one family to another. The work always took place in a circle, and in terms of content, the music is deliberately designed to be inclusive so it would always start with a welcoming activity or welcome song with everybody's names. The framework was loose enough to allow the musicians to tailor their approach to each setting and group of participants, and props such as finger puppets were used to invite and invoke children's responses.

In the Magic Adventure project, play and playfulness underpin everything. Here the adults take their cue from the young participants, creating possibilities for adventure in a space tailor – made for experiencing the world in new ways. Once inside this world, they are immersed in sound and music, boundaries between the adults and children are porous, and the term 'happening' captures the spontaneous and responsive character of the time spent together in this musical world where they are free to explore the environment in their own way and at their own pace.

While it is evident from the information provided by the organisers of both 'Loud and Clear' and 'Magic Adventure' that they serve different purposes, it is worth noting that they both place an emphasis on creating a space which is welcoming, both for the very young children participants and those accompanying them. Great care is taken by the 'Loud and Clear' musicians in advance of their sessions to arrange cushions, rugs, beanbags and soft toys around the room and to put on lamps which add to the atmosphere. In 'Magic Adventure', place is everything and informs the pedagogy throughout, starting with an installation which is safe, stimulating and designed for immersive experiences. It is also interesting to note that they refer very little, if at all, to specific pieces of music or ways of being musical. It is enough for them to be there, and for the workshop leaders to instil in them a sense of trust in the process, and to feel at home in the world. Everything springs from this.

In the third example, the Minute of Listening experience is designed around classroom teachers and framed within a specific time period within which they can explore new musical horizons with their young learners. It is worth noting that this initiative differs from the listenership paradigm discussed in earlier chapters. Where the listenership paradigm is concerned with listening to music, the Minute of Listening wants us to engage with sounds. It is premised on expanding rather than contracting horizons for children (and adults), and circumvents the need to focus on presenting a canon of 'great works' by exploring sound on its own terms and in a variety of imaginative spaces. There is no reference to the creation of a musical world that is safe, or comfortable, as we've noted in respect of both 'Loud and Clear' and 'Magic Adventure', both of which carefully curated the place within which the encounters would take place. This is not to say that it is not of relevance, but rather to note that this is not the primary function of 'Minute of Listening'. It is the willingness to take a risk that would appear to be of importance, for both teacher and learner, and the initiative is built from an intention to encourage participants to focus on the listening experience even when it involves moving outside their comfort zone. Finally, with In Harmony, the fourth example, we see the intention to replicate a group music-making setting, to model the real world of professional orchestral players, where rehearsal and practice habits are inculcated at an early stage, with the expectation that the hard work will result in a public performance, and lead to a world of orchestral music making. While the musical world at the heart of this initiative might be familiar to those leading the workshops – the professional instrumental players and the specialist music teachers – it is clear that it is unfamiliar to the young participants enrolled in it. We can see that the initiative depends for its success on more than musical knowledge: bridging the gap between the two worlds requires careful tuning in to the importance of building meaningful and trusting relationships with all of the participants.

Reflection tasks

Consider the starting points for each of the initiatives discussed in the chapter.

Discuss the ways in which initial planning meetings might have been conducted. Who would be involved in making decisions about the aims, objectives and parameters of the project?

Imagine a future conversation you might have with one of the participants about their experience. What might they say?

7
INTO THE FUTURE

This chapter focuses on:

- Reviewing the key themes of the book
- Musicianism, competence and the teacher's dilemma
- The familiar and the familial in music education
- Being and becoming at home in the world

Introduction

This chapter reviews the key themes which formed the basis of each of the preceding chapters and explores the impact of these on ways of thinking about music education and children's musical worlds. We revisit the concepts of music as object and music as activity, pointing to the way in which psychological and sociological perspectives on musical childhood have informed the construction of knowledge bases of each of these, and in doing so focus on competence and belonging, respectively. In arguing that it is time to consider new possibilities for understanding children's musical worlds, we look to the development of the familial alongside the familiar in children's relationship with music.

Construction of a knowledge base around musical competence

We began by taking an historical overview of the relationship between music and education and traced the influences of each on conceptions of music education to reveal two: one which we defined as *music as object* and the other, *music as activity*. In examining each of these more closely, we saw how the first of these lends itself easily to a master–apprentice model of music education recognisable as developing competence as listener, composer and performer.

We can trace the legacy of testing, which originated from experimental psychology in the presentation of listening to music as a competence, particularly where there is a focus on ascribing labels to specific characteristics such as pulse, duration, dynamics, tempo, timbre, texture and structure. This conveys the message to the learner (and teacher) that each of these characteristics exists in its own discrete state, within parameters that can be identified, discussed and labelled using designated pairs of adjectives (such as loud–soft to indicate changes in dynamics, high–low to indicate change in pitch, fast–slow to indicate change in tempo and so on). It tends to promote an atomistic approach to music listening: the listener is required to isolate one particular characteristic from the whole piece with little account of, or necessity to consider, the context in which the music is heard or placed by the listener, or to how one musical characteristic might belong to, or act within, a network of other inter-related aspects of the music. It reinforces the idea of music as object, music education as aesthetic education, the act of listening *to* as listening *for*, and equates musical knowledge with becoming familiar with, or knowing about, music. In other words, the learners have no part in the formation of this knowledge, but simply must concern themselves with acquiring the knowledge, the skill, or the ability to discern the rules of the game using formal definitions of concepts, devised by others (composer, theorist, teacher).

Whereas the process of familiarising children with music as object through the development of listenership has taken root in children's music education, the history of composing in the musical worlds of children's education is more patchy. Broadly speaking, two distinct forms of composition are discernible in music education, one concerned with creating, the other with recreating. Of these, the second appears to be more prevalent, with its focus on the acquisition of expert constructions of knowledge and skills, and on replication of prescribed practices, compositional techniques or procedures. Following Spitzer (2004), we can see how composition can be framed within theoretical traditions where the processes of reception and creation look back to Bernhard's metaphor of a cosmological 'ladder to heaven' (gradus ad parnassum), Matteson's metaphor of rhetoric using disposition, elaboration and decoration to mirror the composition of a speech, or Koch's generative model of language. Within a framework such as this, composing is about becoming familiar with the steps needed to acquire a technique or ability by following the steps, or learning the rules necessary to replicate a model. What is less commonplace is attention to how we move from the unknown to the known, experiencing time, body and space in relation to each other, and finding ways of learning through improvising and composing to shape the direction of each.

The development of performance skills is perhaps the most widely recognised as the cornerstone of a music curriculum for children where there is a long tradition of an instructional model of teaching. Typically, this involves adults choosing for children music from a set of prescribed pieces, preparing them in advance for performance in spaces which are unfamiliar to the young children. These can be presented to the children as wonderful opportunities and there is no doubt that for many children they are, particularly where the hard work culminates in presentations for audiences familiar to them, namely those in their networks of family and friends. It is fair to say, however, that evidence of the success of this mode of engagement in music making tends to be anecdotal, or based on small samples which are not necessarily representative. On occasions where children are presented as candidates for examination under what we would recognise as laboratory conditions, the relationship between the performer and the audience is more formal, and children are trained to demonstrate their mastery in a battery of tests ranging from aural tests and sight reading using standard notation to scales and arpeggios. Measurement of success of these experiences is easier to quantify, particularly when grades and scoring systems are used as evidence of achievement.

The value of a model of music education such as this, concerned with the production of competent performers, is signalled to all those involved in education of young children when it is enshrined in curriculum documents to the extent that visiting peripatetic teachers are employed through the school or music service to provide individual or small group instrumental lessons in the primary school.

If a musical world created from behaviours predominantly found in western classical music traditions – listenership, composing and performance practice – is presented to children as *the* musical world available to them, with no reference to alternatives, it provides only a partial account of what is possible and what can be imagined. These behaviours can be standardised in the field of education through curriculum, with norms and expectations for development structured around them, legitimising a culture of testing as a means by which to appraise children's efforts in music, and to shape the content and manner of what should be taught.

In the English context, for example, the national plan for music education (Department for Education 2011c; see also Department for Education 2021a; 2021b) aspires to create opportunities for all children to play a musical instrument. On the face of it this is surely a worthy and worthwhile aspiration. On closer inspection, however, it could be said that it takes for granted the fact that performance on a musical instrument is central to music education in school. It has become the norm within the system, such that the class teacher is released from classroom duties at the time of the music lesson, abdicating responsibility for music education to the visiting teacher, and using that time to attend to other duties.

Musicality, competence and the purpose of education

Gert Biesta (2013) cautions us against taking on board the notion of competence unquestioningly. Writing about teaching and teacher education, he notes a move towards one particular way of thinking and talking about teaching and teacher education to the extent that it has become a hegemony, and begins to monopolise thinking and talking. '[I]f there is no alternative discourse, if a particular idea is simply seen as "common sense", then there is a risk that it stops people from thinking at all' (2013, p. 123).

The 'common sense' argument is a compelling and pervasive discourse in matters of music education policy and it is important to reflect on the impact of this on practice. There is a hegemony at the heart of a system of music education when curriculum content focuses primarily on diatonicism (major and minor tonality); when a concept of musicality privileges one musical tradition over another; and when music education becomes synonymous with developing competence in performance and with presenting this for external validation.

When an emphasis on competence underpins the knowledge base for teaching, it can guide the teacher in reaching pre-set goals or targets of attainment, put in place an expectation that what matters in education is training for competence and perpetuate a culture of testing – introduced from the field of experimental psychology – not least in the minds of the classroom teacher whose own formative experiences might lean more towards music as activity than towards music as object.

Consider the impact on teachers presented with a directive or expectation such as the following, taken from England's National Curriculum:

> As pupils progress, they should develop a critical engagement with music, allowing them to compose, and to listen with discrimination to the best in the musical canon. (Department for Education, 2013)

Statements such as these assume a homogeneity of values, of experiences, of preferences or tastes and have a colonising effect on music education. The contents of 'the best in the musical canon' tend to be catalogued according to an atomistic notion of musical knowledge where learning about music moves from the simple to the complex and where the way in which each individual teacher can interpret the curriculum is ignored. This does little to assuage issues of confidence reported among primary teachers, lending weight to their belief that music is something for the few. At a systemic level, where the prospect of offering an alternative is not countenanced, this hegemony represents the 'common sense' approach to teaching and learning, the barometer by which to select children for additional musical participation, the access route to ever diminishing resources in music and the gateway to music as a career, through further or higher education.

Music education and a sense of belonging

We return now to the second perspective, that of music as an activity where human relationships are central. Here we drew from Small's ideas about 'musicking' and Blacking's call to rethink the way we have allowed western classical performance practice of presenting music for reception by a listener in audience to be presented as a universal. If we take their ideas on board, we can begin to see that the environment where composer–performer–audience exist independently of each other can be one of many ways of conceptualising music, and not the only one. We can begin to re-imagine the 'audience' as 'performers' insofar as they can also become involved in the recreation of the 'work' of art. We can see that our musicality does not exist in a vacuum but is shaped by the environment around us. We can see how musicality as a psychological construct might be recast and re-imagined in real-world contexts (see the work of Campbell and Marsh).

Using Bronfenbrenner's ecological model, we can see how learning by osmosis (Campbell) can lend itself to a holistic approach towards music education. In his compelling critique of global perspectives on learning and teaching music, and using examples from a range of cultures and traditions, Huib Schippers shows that there is potential to learn from global perspectives on music to rethink music education in terms of content and method. He suggests that, contrary to the idea that education should be about minimising confusion and risk, there are times when confusion is a powerful instrument in learning music (p. 84). He prefers to see an atomistic approach and a holistic approach not as discrete categories, or presented as binary opposites but on a continuum.

> An atomistic/analytic approach corresponds more closely to an emphasis on mono-directional didactic teaching of a 'single truth', while a holistic approach leaves more room for learners to construct their own musical knowing, leading to a more individual approach, even if the body of knowledge (the canon or tradition) is quite closely defined. (p. 85)

This allows us to hold both an instructivist and a constructivist perspective on learning. In the first, the notion of meaning in positivist knowledge is based on propositions, on absolute truths; and in the second, knowledge is interpretivist, the consequence of cognitive and social interaction, where meaning is negotiated among the participants.

We have seen from Chapter 2 that in the context of Brazil, Freire likened education to a banking system where knowledge was commodified like currency, with teachers dispensing it and learners depositing it. Critical pedagogy challenges the practice of describing change in educational terms rooted in measurement and assessment of learner behaviour. Instead it activates the learners to name the world so that they can bring about social change. Hess (2019) takes up this thread and asks us to consider what change looks like from the perspective of social activism. From this perspective music education becomes political as well as educational and cultural. She asks how music education can contribute to changing the social climate (of racism and violence targeted at people who embody difference). Her point is that music learning intrinsically involves exploring social, political, historical and cultural contexts and that musical activism can provide a significant mechanism for music learning.

> How might youth interact with music in music education in ways that validate their experiences and help them to develop their own unique voices? How might such interaction with music education contribute to social change? (2019, p. 4)

Questions such as these remind us that the lived experiences of the learner transcend any boundaries between what takes place in school and outside it. In the context of music, they invite us to enter into conversations with each other about the purpose of music education, provoking further questions:

> (adapting from hooks) 'I thought this was supposed to be a [music] class... [W]hy are we talking so much about [non music issues such as] race or class?' (1994, p. 42)

They remind us too that discussions about whether music education is conceptualised around music as object or music as activity must not be insulated from the world, but nested within it, taking account of the fact that both teacher and learner encounter the world through their experience of music education. Freire's notion of conscientisation is relevant here, promoting as it does the engagement of both teacher and learner in reflection and action – or praxis – in order to understand the world, and from there to change it (Freire, 1970, 1995).

It is worth noting too Biesta's (2022) point, following Roth (2011), that there is something of a paradox around a constructivist metaphor. What matters is not that the outcome is not yet known but that the learner reaches out; it is something given to us: 'it is not a knowing that precedes our reaching out, but rather that our reaching out is called for by the things we encounter' (2022, p. 93). It is the opening ourselves up to the possibility that is crucial here and for Biesta this is where the risk lies, this uncertainty, this vulnerability. This changes the perspective of education as a responsibility of the teacher not only to the learner, but to the world.

Drawing lines, creating spaces

In advancing the notion that curriculum is a way of presenting the world to the learner and of representing the world for the learner, Biesta (2022) suggests that a world-centred education is one where the emphasis moves from the teacher towards the world. The teacher's responsibility is to point the learner to the world. 'This is not to discharge the teacher from his or her responsibilities, but it is to see that the key task of the teacher is to point the student to the world, to (re)direct the student's attention to the world so that it becomes possible, without guarantees of course, that the student may meet that which the world is asking from him or her' (p. 99). It demands that the teacher treats the learner not in an infantile way or as a dependant, the object of the educator's judgement, but encourages them to 'become a subject of their own action, that is, to attend to their own subjectness and their own freedom' (p. 101).

He points to the limitations of words such as 'learning' and 'development', arguing that they are directionless terms. 'To the extent to which the word "learning" has any meaning at all, there is always the need to specify what the learning is *about* and what it is supposed to be *for*' (p. vii).

If we apply this to music education, and to the examples provided in this book, we can ask ourselves: what is the learning about and what is it supposed to be for? In some of the cases our response might be that the learning is about social mobility, and about developing in our learners self-esteem to take their place in a world we have created for them. In others it could be argued that our response is that the learning is about limiting options rather than opening them up, particularly where the learning is for development of expertise in a set of skills which prepare some more than others for a world of music making.

He wants us to approach thinking about education *educationally* (p. vii; my italics), and proposes qualification, socialisation and subjectification as three domains in which educational purposes can be articulated. These he summarises as follows:

> [Q]ualification ... has to do with the acquisition of knowledge, skills, values and dispositions[;] socialization ... has to do with the ways in which, through education, we become part of existing traditions and ways of doing and being[; and] ... subjectification ... has to do with the interest of education in the subjectivity or 'subject-ness' of those we educate. (p. 4)

Education takes place in the here and now. It involves risks for learners and teachers if the purpose of education is to include these three dimensions. These risks are aesthetic risks and require us to move away from the certainty of pre-empting the outcome of children's endeavours, from focusing on getting it right, on effectiveness and on efficiency.

> What we hope for is that, at some point, students will turn back to us and tell us that what we tried to give them was actually quite helpful, meaningful, even if initially it was difficult to receive. At that point we can say that the unidirectional exercise of power transforms into a relationship of authority, where what intervened from outside is authorised by the student – is 'allowed' to be an author, is 'allowed' to speak and have a voice. (p. 56)

It is about creating space for them.

The teacher's dilemma

We now ask ourselves about teacher autonomy and freedom in a system which, though setting out to enable and empower teachers, may disable and disempower some of them. This comes about through reinforcing the stereotype of music as object, privileging the presentational over the participative and leaning towards an emphasis on skill acquisition.

Where the outcome being sought is demonstrable competence in performance, it stands to reason that teaching needs to concern itself with whatever is required to bring about competence in the learner. At worst, where the focus on the outcome overshadows all considerations other than meeting norms of improvement, teachers – and those making decisions which lead to this situation – may overlook the value of assessing the effort of each learner on their own merit in favour of satisfying themselves that what the learners produce meets externally imposed norms and standards. In bringing about mastery of a set of skills in the learner, they may pay less attention to the prior experience of those whose skills are being developed, or to how the instruction they provide maps onto the learner's previous encounters with music. Framed in this way, music education becomes directive and brings to mind Jorgensen's image of a factory outlined in Chapter 1: 'It regards the transition of wisdom and knowledge as a one way process from the teacher to the student, where the teacher gives and the student passively receives' (2011, p. 98).

One of the most vocal critics of this practice is Thomas Regelski. Regelski's use of the term 'musicianism' (2012) denotes the practice whereby musical choices and values are given more weight than educational options and values. It is ideological, hegemonic, dogmatic and self-serving:

> ideological in the sense that it chooses only what suits it, a partial view of the child, focused only on those who can and ignoring or dismission those who can't; imposed as being good for everyone, whether they like it or not;
>
> hegemonic in that the music teachers can dictate the rules of the game, the choice of music, the manner in which the teacher–learner roles are played on;
>
> dogmatic by sending the message that it's the only and best show in town; and

self-serving in that the musical requirements of the teacher are served, in effect enabling the teacher to replicate the training they had in their own formative experience. (2012, pp. 22–3)

We have seen in earlier chapters how projects are devised for young musicians which take music as art object, musicianism and presentational performance as the norm and we must be mindful of the balance of 'voice' in discussions about musicality and musical worlds of children. When claims are made for the success of such projects, we must listen out for the quiet voices, or notice the absent or silent voices of those young learners who do not take part in the projects. If competence is the outcome, Regelski (2017) suggests that the teacher will focus on those learners who demonstrate the capacity to bring about success on the task. He argues that where this becomes the norm, those who do not or cannot meet this are left behind.

Tasks structured around an expertise paradigm are those in which, Regelski notes, the musically competent visiting peripatetic teachers are themselves invested. 'Music teachers may easily succumb to the notion that the music of school music – the 'good' music with which the music teacher is most familiar and competent – is somehow special, or is more valuable than the music in the larger music world outside of school' (2012, p. 12).

Wayne Bowman (2007) uses the metaphor of a cycle to demonstrate how this notion of 'good' music is perpetuated by music teachers themselves and describes how this works in practice:

[s]tart with an understanding of music derived from, and suited to one particular mode of musical engagement and practice. [Then we c]raft a definition of musicianship derived from its basic tenets and demonstrable primarily on instruments that have evolved in its service. [We p]rivilege curricula and pedagogies that serve to nurture that kind of musi-cianship[, s]elect students for advanced study on the basis of criteria well-suited to these modes of practice. [Teachers are hired] to serve the needs of these students and … suc-cess [is assessed] in terms of the extent to which the norms and values of that tradition and its conventions are preserved. (2007, p. 116)

Regelski goes further, to suggest that 'teachers who are mainly serving their own musical needs can be largely unconcerned with students who fall behind or drop out, rational-izing that they are unworthy or uncommitted' (2012, pp. 11–12) Teachers who work from an education perspective will know that the learners who are falling behind need extra support if they are to meet the standards imposed by the teacher in this scenario. What tends to happen in this situation is that these learners will walk away from what is on offer at the earliest opportunity. We need to appreciate that the risks involved for teachers in resisting the status quo are considerable, particularly where calls to transform teaching and learning are made in classroom settings so that the learning experience is inclusive.

Let's face it: most of us were taught in classrooms where styles of teachings reflected the notion of a single norm of thought and experience, which we were encouraged to believe was universal. (hooks, p. 35)

The prospect of approaching a subject such as classroom music in multiple ways and with multiple reference points brings with it the possibility of confrontation, of losing control, and fear of changing custom and practice. If we move away from tried and tested ideas about music in education, we must surely need to have something on hand to put in its place. It is not an accident that the music as object metaphor and education as training model have persisted in practice, and alternatives to the canon have not had much traction. We have seen examples of resistance to change in an earlier chapter: Stravinsky's attempt to create new sonic spaces in the field of western classical music over a century ago; Cage's attempt to challenge the listener to reimagine the boundaries between 'music' and 'nonmusic'. Yet a concern with ideas about reimagining the parameters of sound has remained peripheral in much of what happens in music education.

We have seen that new materialism offers a new musical world, one which is concerned more with environment – the relational aspect of being in the world – than with scenery – or looking at something from the outside in (Voegelin, 2019). In the case of John Cage's *4'33"*, although 'silence' was constructed by the non-sounded music, the event itself was not silent. The sounds in the environment intruded and took over the space created such that the audience became part of the sonic event. The piece becomes fluid then to the extent that there's no definitive version of it. That is the point. In this respect, Cage's challenge to the audience to listen to the silence in his *4'33"* can be seen as an invitation to reimagine the sonic world as relational. Likewise with regard to the sonic sensibilities of the audience who were allegedly so shocked and outraged at the crossing of a line at the first performance of Stravinsky's *Rite of Spring*, if we were to reimagine it from a new materialist perspective, we would not want to separate the sounds of Stravinsky's music presented by the musicians – the art object – from the sounds made in the hall by the audience – its reception: indeed the entire experience as it unfolded would need to be reconceptualised to decentre the art object, dispensing with the distinction between presentation and reception (Schafer, 1967; Shannon, 2019).

It is clear that both events crossed a line between what was considered to belong inside and outside the boundaries of music. With the first performance of Stravinsky's piece, we can find reports that the audience was expecting something other than what it got and had no reference point for what was presented to them. We could say that they were conditioned to hear music within a particular frame of sonic reference and what they encountered fell outside this.

It is time now to look at the metaphor running through the book, namely that of the world, in respect of children's music education. We have seen a musical world created by adults for children in the formal education system, with music conceptualised as a soundworld from western classical instruments using dimensions of pitch relations.

We have seen how children can create a musical world independently of adults, where they learn with and from each other, moving between roles and responsibilities. We have seen how children explore the soundworld around them, in environments that are physical and immediate, and imagined and virtual. We have seen how adults create opportunities for children to encounter music through projects such as Loud and Clear, Magic Adventure, Minute of Listening and In Harmony. Each is an ecology of learning, a place for children to encounter music 'just beyond the classroom' (Knapp, 1996). We can consider each of these on its own terms, each one with its own *raison d'être* and distinct identity, each one serving the needs of a particular community. The challenge is to find a way for each community to exist in its own world but without losing touch with, or becoming adrift from other communities.

David Gruenewald (2003) proposes a critical pedagogy of place as a way of connecting what happens within the classroom with what happens outside it. He argues that there are two broad and inter-related objectives for erasing the lines between them and linking them to the larger landscape of cultural and ecological politics: decolonisation and reinhabitation.

> From an educational perspective, it means unlearning much of what dominant culture and schooling teaches, and learning more socially just and ecologically sustainable ways of being in the world. (p. 9)

Empathy and exploration are considered to be valued learning experiences in themselves, and a critical pedagogy of place means developing empathy alongside exploration, challenging 'placeless' standardised curricula and promoting the well-being of place.

> Developing a critical pedagogy of place means challenging each other to read the texts of our own lives and to ask constantly what needs to be transformed and what needs to be conserved. In short, it means making a place for the cultural, political, economic and ecological dynamics of places whenever we talk about the purpose and practice of learning. (pp. 10–11)

In this sense, while music education is about becoming familiar with music through encountering it as object within a composer–listener–performer paradigm, or within the participative nature of musicking – a human activity – both of which we have explored in this book, or in some other framework or dimension which allows for us to conceive of or imagine soundworlds not yet imagined or imaginable, it is also about recognising that such encounters are not placeless – and education can be concerned with developing a familial relationship with ourselves and our world (see Nind and Hewett, 1994/2005; Frith et al. 2010). It involves knowing ourselves, our world and our place within it. This place can be real or imagined, virtual or augmented. It is wherever we locate ourselves. For teachers and learners, music education can thus be about learning to know your place, finding your place and knowing it as a place where, following Biesta (2022), you can be at home in the world.

Reflection tasks

Consider how Gruenewald (2003) makes a connection between 'decolonization' and 'reinhabitation':

> If reinhabitation involves learning to live well socially and ecologically in places that have been disrupted and injured, decolonization involves learning to recognize disruption and injury and to address their causes. (p. 9)

Discuss how the metaphor of place – colonising and inhabiting – might relate to music education and to children's musical worlds.

REFERENCES

Allsup, R. (2015). 'Music teacher quality and the problem of routine expertise'. *Philosophy of Music Education Review* 23(1), 5–24.

Anderson, J., Little, J. and Mooney, E. n.d. Loud & Clear Foster and Adoptive Family Learning. *Early Years Evaluation* 2013–14.

Arts Council (n.d.). In Harmony. www.artscouncil.org.uk/music-education-hubs/harmony.

Bakan, M. (2018). *Music & autism: Speaking for ourselves*. Oxford: Oxford University Press.

Beardsley, M. (1975). *Aesthetics from classical Greek to the present; a short history*. New York: Macmillan.

Bentley, A. (1966). *Measures of musical abilities*. London: Harrap & Co. Ltd.

Bernstein, B. (2000). *Pedagogy, symbolic control and identity. Theory, research, critique*. Revised edition. Oxford: Rowman & Littlefield.

Biesta, G. (2013). *The beautiful risk of education*. London: Paradigm Publishers.

Biesta, G. (2022). *World-centred education: A view for the present*. Oxford: Routledge.

Blacking, J. (1967). *Venda children's songs: A study in ethnomusicological analysis*. Chicago, IL: University of Chicago Press.

Blacking, J. (1976). *How musical is man?* London: Faber and Faber.

Blacking, J. (1987). *A common sense view of all music: Reflections on Percy Grainger's contribution to ethnomusicology and music education*. Cambridge: Cambridge University Press.

Bourdieu, P. (1977). *Outline of a theory of practice. Volume 16 of Cambridge Studies in Social and Cultural Anthropology* (trans. Nice). Cambridge: Cambridge University Press.

Bourdieu, P., and Passeron, J.-C. (1990). *Reproduction in education, society and culture* (2nd ed.) (R. trans. Nice). London: Sage Publications, Inc.

Bowman, W. (2007). 'Who is the "We"? Rethinking professionalism in music education'. *Action, Criticism, and Theory for Music Education* 6(4), 109–31.

Bronfenbrenner, U. (1979). *The ecology of human development*. Cambridge, MA: Harvard University Press.

Bruner, J. (1966). *Toward a theory of instruction*. Cambridge, MA: Harvard University Press.

Budd, M. (1995). *Music and the emotions: The philosophical theories*. International Library of Philosophy. London: Routledge.

Burton, S. (2021). 'Digital music play in early childhood'. In G. Greher and S. Burton (eds), *Creative music making at your fingertips: A mobile technology guide for music educators.* Oxford: Oxford University Press. pp. 16–28.

Cameron, C., Moss, P. and Petrie, P. (2021). 'Towards a social pedagogic approach for social care'. *International Journal of Social Pedagogy* 10(1), 7. https://doi.org/10.14324/111.444. ijsp.2021.v10.x.007.

Campbell, P. (2010). *Songs in their heads: Music and its meaning in children's lives,* 2nd ed. Oxford: Oxford University Press.

Campbell, P. (2011). 'Music enculturation: Sociocultural influences and meanings of children's experiences in and through music'. In M. Barrett (ed.), *A cultural psychology of music education.* Oxford: Oxford University Press. pp. 61–81.

Ceraso, S. (2018). *Sounding composition: Multimodal pedagogies for embodied listening.* Pittsburgh, PA: University of Pittsburgh Press.

Clark, T., Williamon, A. and Aksentijevic, A. (2012). 'Musical imagery and imagination: the function, measurement, and applicaton of imagery skills for performance'. In D. Hargreaves, D. Miell and R. Macdonald (eds)., *Musical imaginations: Multidisciplinary perspectives on creativity, performance, and perception.* Oxford: Oxford University Press. pp. 351–65.

Colwell, R. (1968). *Music achievement tests.* Urbana, IL: Follett Publications.

Cook, N. (2007). 'Imagining things: mind into music (and back again)'. In I. Roth (ed)., *Imaginative minds: Proceedings of the British Academy.* Oxford: Oxford University Press. pp. 123–46.

Cooke, D. (1959). *The language of music.* Oxford: Oxford University Press.

Copland, A. (1952). *Music and imagination. The Charles Eliot Norton Lectures 1951–1952.* Cambridge, MA: Harvard University Press.

Cox, G. (2002). 'A house divided?' Music education in the United Kingdom during the Schools Council Era of the 1970s. *Journal of Historical Research in Music Education* 22(2), 160–75.

Cox, G. (2015). 'Historical perspectives'. In G. McPherson (ed.), *The child as musician: A handbook of musical development.* Oxford: Oxford University Press. pp. 523–37.

Davies, S. (2011). *Musical understandings and other essays on the philosophy of music.* Oxford: Oxford University Press.

Dennis, B. (1970). *Experimental music in schools.* Oxford: Oxford University Press.

Dennis, B. (1975). *Projects in sound.* London: Universal Edition.

Department for Education (2011a). *Music education in England. A review by Darren Henley for the Department for Education and the Department for Culture, Media and Sport.* Crown Publications, accessed at https://www.gov.uk/government/publications/music-education-in-england-a-review-by-darren-henley-for-the-department-for-education-and-the-department-for-culture-media-and-sport (15 February 2022).

Department for Education (2011b). *Music education in England. The Government response to Darren Henley's review of music education.* Crown Publications, accessed at https://www.gov.uk/government/publications/music-education-in-england-the-government-response-to-darren-henleys-review-of-music-education (15 February 2022).

Department for Education (2011c). *The importance of music. A national plan for music education*. Crown Publications, accessed at https://www.gov.uk/government/publications/the-importance-of-music-a-national-plan-for-music-education (15 February 2022).

Department for Education (2013). *Music programmes of study: Key stages 1 and 2. National curriculum in England*. London: Department for Education.

Department for Education (2021). *Statutory framework for the early years foundation stage: Setting the standards for learning, development and care for children from birth to five*. London: Department for Education.

Department for Education (2021a). *Music education: report on the call for evidence conducted February–March 2021*. London: Department for Education.

Department for Education (2021b). *Model music curriculum: key stages 1–3. Non-statutory guidance for the national curriculum in England*. London: Department for Education.

Dunn, R. (1997). 'Creative thinking and music listening'. *Research in Music Education* 8, 42–55.

Dzansi, M. (2004). 'Playground music pedagogy of Ghanaian children'. *Research in Music Education* 22, 83–92.

Eklund Koza, J. (2021). 'Destined to fail'. Carl Seashore's world of eugenics, psychology, education, and music. University of Michigan Press.

Elkoshi, R. (2015), 'Children's invented notations and verbal response to a piano work by Claude Debussy'. *Music Education Research* 17(2), 179–200.

Emmerson, S. (2011). 'Music imagination technology'. Keynote Address. In *Proceedings of the International Computer Music Conference, Huddersfield*. San Francisco, CA: ICMA. pp. 365–72.

Emmerson, S. (2019). Playing the inner ear: performing the imagination. In M. Grimshaw-Aagaard, M. Walther-Hansen and M. Knakkergaard (eds), *The Oxford handbook of sound and imagination, Volume 2*. Oxford: Oxford University Press. pp. 258–78.

Firth, G., Berry, R. and Irvine, C. (2010). *Understanding intensive interaction: Contexts and concepts for professionals and families*. London: Jessica Kingsley Publishers.

Forrai, K. (1988). *Music in preschool* (trans. and adapted by Jean Sinor). Budapest: Corvina.

Freire, P. (1970). *Pedagogy of the oppressed* (trans. M.B. Ramos). New York, NY: Herder and Herder.

Freire, P. (1995). *Pedagogy of hope. reliving pedagogy of the oppressed*. New York, NY: Continuum.

Gabrielsson, A. (2002). 'Emotion perceived and emotion felt: same or different?' *Musicae Scientiae Special Issue 2001–2002* 5(1), 123–47.

Gallagher, M., Prior, J., Needham, M. and Holmes, R. (2017). 'Listening differently: A pedagogy for expanded listening'. *British Educational Research Journal* 43(6), 1246–65.

Gordon, E. (1965). *Musical aptitude profile*. Boston, MA: Houghton Mifflin.

Gordon, E. (1970). *Iowa tests of music literacy*. Iowa City, IA: Bureau of Educational Research and Service.

Gould, S. (1980). *Ontogeny and phylogeny*. Cambridge, MA: The Belknap Press of Harvard University Press.

Gruenewald, D. (2003). 'The best of both worlds: a critical pedagogy of place'. *Educational Researcher* 32(4), 3–12.

Hallam, S. and Burns, S. (2017). *Research into support for musical progression for young people from In Harmony programmes and other disadvantaged communities.* www.artscouncil.org.uk/sites/default/files/downloadfile/In_harmony_Final_report.pdf.

Hallam, S. and Burns, S. (2018). Research into support for musical progression for young people from In Harmony programmes and other disadvantaged communities. *Phase Two Research: Action research and case studies.* www.artscouncil.org.uk/sites/default/files/download-file/IH_Musical_Progression_PhaseTwoReport_Dec18_0.pdf.

Hanslick, E. (1854). *Du Beau dans la Musique.* Paris: Macquet (1986 ed., Paris: Christian Bourgois Editeur). English trans. G. Cohen (1974) *The Beautiful in Music.* New York, NY: Da Capo Press.

Harris, P. (2000). *The work of the imagination.* London: Wiley-Blackwell.

Haselbach, B. (ed.) (2011). *Texts on theory and practice of Orff-Schulwerk. Volume 1 Basic texts on the Orff-Schulwerk: Reports from the years 1932–2010.* Mainz: Schott Music.

Hess, J. (2019). *Music education for social change. Constructing an activist music education.* New York, NY: Routledge.

Holst, I. (1952). 'Britten and the young'. In D. Mitchell and H. Keller (eds), *Benjamin Britten, a commentary on his works from a group of specialists.* London: Rockliff, 268–278.

Honing, H. (2009). *Musical cognition: A science of listening.* London: Transaction.

hooks, b. (1994). *Teaching to transgress: Education as the practice of freedom.* London: Routledge.

Huhtinen-Hildén, L. and Pitt, J. (2018). *Taking a learner-centred approach to music education: Pedagogical pathways.* London: Routledge.

inspire-music (n.d.). *Loud and Clear – early years.* https://inspire-music.org/component/content/article?id=66:loud-and-clear-early-years.

Jorgensen, E. (2011). *Pictures of music education.* Bloomington, IN: Indiana University Press.

Kanellopoulos, P. (2008). '"For us it is important, but to other people it might seem foolish": conceptualising "child music"'. In B. Roberts (ed.), *Sociological explorations. Proceedings of the 5th international symposium on the sociology of music education. Memorial University of Newfoundland.* St John's Newfoundland: The Binder's Press. pp. 217–36.

Kendell, I. (1974). *Schools Council/University of Reading Research and Development Report 'Music education of young children'* (Director Dr Arnold Bentley). Interim report. June 1974.

Kenny, A. (2010). *A new history of western philosophy.* Oxford: Oxford University Press.

Knapp, C. (1996). *Just beyond the classroom.* Charleston, WV: Eric Press.

Kodály, Z. (1974). *Selected writings of Zoltan Kodály.* (trans. Halápy and Macnicol). London: Boosey & Hawkes.

Kodály, Z. (2007). *Visszatekintés* [Selected Writings], Vol. II (ed. F. Bónis, trans. L. Nemes). Budapest: Argumentum.

Kress, G. (2010). *Multimodality: a social semiotic approach to contemporary communication.* Abingdon: Routledge Press.

Kreutz, G., Ott, U. and Wehrum, S. (2006). 'Cerebral correlates of musically-induced emotions: an fMRI-study'. In M. Baroni et al. (eds), Proceedings of the 9th International Conference on Music Perception and Cognition (ICMPC), Bologna, 22–26 August 2006.

Kreutz, G., and Lotze, M, (2007). 'Neuroscience of music and emotion'. In W. Gruhn and F. Rauscher (eds), Neuroscience in music pedagogy. New York: Nova Science Publishers Inc. pp. 143–67.

Kullenberg, T. (2014). 'Signing and singing – children in teaching dialogues'. Unpublished dissertation, University of Gothenburg.

Lagerlöf, P. and Wallerstedt, C. (2019). '"I don't even dare to do it": Problematising the image of the competent and musical child'. Music Education Research 21(1), 86–98.

Lave, J. and Wenger, E. (1991). Situated learning: Legitimate peripheral participation. Manchester: Manchester University Press.

Lewis, J. (2020). 'How children listen: multimodality and its implications for K–12 music education and music teacher education'. Music Education Research 22(4), 373–87.

Littleton, K. and Mercer, N. (2012). 'Communication, collaboration, and creativity: How musicians negotiate a collective "sound"'. In D. Hargreaves, D. Miell and R. Macdonald (eds), Musical imaginations: Multidisciplinary perspectives on creativity, performance, and perception. Oxford: Oxford University Press. pp. 233–41.

London, J. (2002). 'Some theories of emotion in music and their implications for research in music psychology'. Musicae Scientiae Special Issue 2001–2002 5(1), 23–36.

Lum, C.H. and Dairianathan, E. (2012). 'Reflexive and reflective perspectives of musical childhoods in Singapore'. In P. Shehan-Campbell and T. Wiggins (eds), The Oxford handbook of children's musical cultures. Oxford: Oxford University Press. pp. 332–49.

Lundqvist, L.O., Carlsson, F., Hilmersson, P. and Juslin, P. (2009). 'Emotional responses to music: experience, expression, and physiology'. Psychology of Music 37, 61–90.

Mackinlay, E. (2012). 'The musical worlds of Aboriginal children at Burrulula and Darwin in the Northern Territory of Australia'. In P. Shehan-Campbell and T. Wiggins (eds), The Oxford handbook of children's musical cultures. Oxford: Oxford University Press. pp. 315–31.

Magic Acorns (2020). Homepage. www.magicacorns.co.uk/.

Magic Adventure (2013). Homepage. www.magic-adventure.co.uk/.

Marsh, K. (1995). 'Children's singing games: composition in the playground?' Research Studies in Music Education 4(1), 2–11.

Marsh, K. (2008). The musical playground: Global tradition and change in children's songs and games. Oxford: Oxford University Press.

Marsh, K. (2011). 'Meaning-making through musical play: Cultural psychology of the playground'. In M. Barrett (ed.), A cultural psychology of music education. Oxford: Oxford University Press. pp. 41–60.

Marsh, K. and Young, S. (2006). 'Musical play'. In G. McPherson (ed), The child as musician. Oxford: Oxford University Press. pp. 289–310.

Mellers, W. (1964a). 'Music for 20th century children 1: Magic and ritual in the junior school'. Musical Times, May, 342–5.

Mellers, W. (1964b). 'Music for 20th century children 2: From magic to drama'. *Musical Times*, June, 421–7.

Meyer, L. (1956). *Emotion and meaning in music*. Chicago, IL: University of Chicago Press.

Minute of Listening (2022). Homepage. www.minuteoflistening.org.

Mitchell, D. and Keller, H. (eds) (1952). *Benjamin Britten: a commentary on his works from a group of specialists*. London: Rockliff Publishing Corporation Limited.

Morrison, S. (2009). *The people's artist – Prokofiev's Soviet years*. New York, NY: Oxford University Press.

Nachnanovitch, S. (1990). *Free play: improvisation in life and art*. New York, NY: TarcherPerigree.

Nannyonga-Tamusuza, S. (2012). 'Girlhood songs, musical tales, and musical games as strategies for socialisation into womanhood among the Baganda of Uganda'. In P. Shehan-Campbell and T. Wiggins (eds), *The Oxford handbook of children's musical cultures*. Oxford: Oxford University Press. pp. 114–30.

Nattiez, J. (1990). *Music and discourse: Towards a semiology of music* (trans. Carolyn Abbate). Princeton, NJ: Princeton University Press.

Nemes, L. (2017). '"Let the whole world rejoice!" Choral music education: The Kodály perspective'. In F. Abrahams and P. Head (eds), *The Oxford handbook of choral pedagogy*. Oxford: Oxford University Press. pp. 87–104.

Nind, M. and Hewett, D. (1994/2005). *Access to communication: Developing the basics of communication with people with severe developmental disabilities through intensive interaction*. London: David Fulton.

Ockelford, A. (2013). *Applied musicology: using zygonic theory to inform music education, therapy, and psychology research*. New York, NY: Oxford University Press.

Ockelford, A. (2019). 'A different way of imagining sound: Probing the inner auditory worlds of some children on the autism spectrum'. In M. Grimshaw-Aagaard, M. Walther-Hansen and M. Knakkergaard (eds), *The Oxford Handbook of Sound and Imagination, Volume 2*. Oxford: Oxford University Press. pp. 409–26.

O'Neill, S. (2012). 'Becoming a music learner: towards a theory of transformative music engagement'. In G. McPherson and G. Welch (eds), *The Oxford handbook of sound and imagination, volume 1*. Oxford: Oxford University Press. pp. 163–88.

Paynter, J. and Aston, P. (1970). *Sound and silence*. Cambridge: Cambridge University Press.

Pearson, D. (2007). 'Mental imagery and creative thought'. In I. Roth, (ed.), *Imaginative minds: Proceedings of the British Academy*. Oxford: Oxford University Press, pp. 187–212.

Pflederer, M. (1964). 'The responses of children to musical tasks embodying Piaget's principle of conservation'. *Journal of Research in Music Education* 12, 251–68.

Piaget, J. (1952). *The origins of intelligence in the child*. London: Routledge and Kegan Paul.

Pieridou Skoutella, A. (2019). *Small musical worlds in the Mediterranean: Ethnicity, globalization and Greek Cypriot children's musical identities*. London: Routledge.

Regelski, T. (2012). 'Musicianism and the ethics of school music'. *Action, Criticism, and Theory for Music Education* 11(1), 7–42.

Reichling, M. (1997). 'Music, imagination, and play'. *Journal of Aesthetic Education* 31(1), 41–55.

Rinsema, R. (2018). 'De-sacralising the European: music appreciation (then) and music listening (now)'. *Music Education Research* 20(4), 480–9.

Root-Bernstein, M. (2013). 'The creation of imaginary worlds'. In M. Taylor (ed.), *The Oxford handbook of the development of imagination*. Oxford: Oxford University Press. pp. 417–38.

Roth, I. (2007). *Imaginative minds: Proceedings of the British Academy*. Oxford: Oxford University Press.

Roth, W. (2011). *Passability: At the limits of the constructivist metaphor*. Dordrecht: Springer.

Schafer, R.M. (1965). *The composer in the classroom*. Toronto: BMI.

Schafer, R.M. (1967). *Ear cleaning*. Toronto: BMI.

Schafer, R.M. (1994). *The soundscape: Our sonic environment and the tuning of the world*. Rochester, VT: Destiny Books.

Schippers, H. (2010). *Facing the music: Shaping music education from a global perspective*. Oxford: Oxford University Press.

Seashore, C. (1919a). *The psychology of musical talent, XVI*. New York, NY: Silver, Burdett.

Seashore, C. (1919b). *Manual of instructions and interpretations of measures of musical talent*. Chicago, IL: C.H. Stoelting.

Seashore, C. (1938). *Psychology of music*. New York: McGraw Hill.

Serafine, M. (1980). 'Piagetian research in music'. *Bulletin of the Council for Research in Music Education* 62, 1–21.

Shannon, D. (2019). '"What could be feminist about sound studies?": (in)Audibility in young children's soundwalking'. *Journal of Public Pedagogies* 4. https://doi.org/10.15209/jpp.1178.

Shehan Campbell, P. (2008). *Musician and teacher, an orientation to music education*. London: Norton and Company.

Silvey, R. and Mackeith, S. (1988). 'The paracosm: A special form of fantasy'. In D.C. Morrison (ed.), *Organizing early experience: imagination and cognition in childhood*. Amityville, NY: Baywood. pp. 173–97.

Small, C. (1998). *Musicking: The meanings of performing and listening*. Middletown, CT: Wesleyan University Press.

Small, C. and Walser, R. (1996). *Music, society, education. Revised edition*. Hanover, NH: Wesleyan.

Spitzer, M. (2004). *Metaphor and musical thought*. Chicago, IL: University of Chicago Press.

Stakelum, M. (2008). Creating a musical world in the classroom: application of a Bourdieuan approach towards understanding teacher practice. *British Journal of Music Education*, 25(1), 91–102.

Stakelum, M. and Baker, D. (2013). 'The MaPS project: Mapping teachers' conceptions of musical development'. In M. Stakelum (ed.), *Developing the musician: contemporary perspectives on teaching and learning*. SEMPRE Studies in the Psychology of Music. Farnham: Ashgate. pp. 135–54.

Swanwick, K. (1988). *Music, mind and education*. London: Routledge.

Swanwick, K. (1994). *Musical knowledge. Intuition, analysis and music education*. London: Routledge.

Swanwick, K. (1999). *Teaching music musically*. London: Routledge.

Swanwick, K, and Tillman, J. (1986). 'The sequence of musical development: a study of children's compositions'. *British Journal of Music Education* 3(3), 305–39.

Szönyi, E. (1983). *Kodály's principles in practice. An approach to music education through the Kodály method* (trans. John Weissman). Budapest: Corvina Kiado.

Tomlinson, G. (2020). 'Posthumanism'. In T. McAuley, N. Nielsen, J. Levinson and A. Phillips-Hutton (eds), *The Oxford handbook of western music and philosophy*. Oxford: Oxford University Press. pp. 415–34.

Turino, T. (2008). *Music as social life. The politics of participation*. Chicago, IL: The University of Chicago Press.

Tuuri, K. and Peltola, H. (2014). 'Imagining between ourselves: a group interview approach in exploring listening experiences'. In M. Grimshaw and M. Walther-Hansen (eds), *Proceedings of the 9th audio mostly: A conference on interaction with sound*, 6:1–6:8., NY New York, NY: ACM Press.

Tuuri, K. and Peltola, H. (2019). 'Building worlds together with sound and music: Imagination as an active engagement between ourselves'. In M. Grimshaw-Aagaard, M. Walther-Hansen and M. Knakkergaard (eds), *The Oxford handbook of sound and imagination, Volume 1*. Oxford: Oxford University Press. pp. 345–60.

Upitis, R. (2019). *This too is music*, 2nd ed. Oxford: Oxford University Press.

Vernon, P. (ed.) (1970). *Creativity: Selected readings*. Harmondsworth: Penguin Books.

Vestad, I. (2014). 'Children's subject positions in discourses of music in everyday life: Rethinking conceptions of the child in and for music education'. *Action, Criticism, and Theory for Music Education* 13(1), 248–78.

Voegelin, S. (2019). 'Sonic materialism: hearing the Arche-Sonic'. In M. Grimshaw-Aagaard, M. Walther-Hansen and M. Knakkergaard (eds), *The Oxford handbook of sound and imagination, Volume 2*. Oxford: Oxford University Press. pp. 559–76.

Vygotsky, L. (1934/1986). *Thought and language* (rev. and trans. A. Kozulin). Cambridge, MA: Harvard University Press.

Webster, P. (1987). 'Conceptual bases for creative thinking in music'. In C. Peery, I. Peery and T. Draper (eds), *Music and child development*. New York: Springer-Verlag pp. 158–74.

Westerkamp, H. (2007). 'Soundwalking'. In A. Carlyle (ed.), *Autumn leaves: Sound and the environment in artistic practice*. Paris: Double Entendre. p. 49. https://www.basw.co.uk/system/files/resources/basw_100448-3_0.pdf

Wing, H.D. (1961). *Wing standardised tests of musical intelligence*. Windsor: NFER Publishing.

Wishart, T. (1996). *On sonic art*, rev. ed. (ed. S. Emmerson). Contemporary Music Studies, Volume 12. Abingdon: Routledge.

Woods, P. (2019). 'Conceptions of teaching in and through noise: A study of experimental musicians' beliefs'. *Music Education Research* 21(4), 459–68.

Zerull, D. (1993). *The role of musical imagination in the musical listening experience*. Unpublished doctoral dissertation, Northwestern University.

Zimmerman, M. (1970). 'Percept and concept: Implications of Piaget'. *Music Educators Journal* 56(6), 49–50.

INDEX

4'33" (Cage), 27, 103

acoustic definition of music as sound, 24
active listening, 43
adoptive parents, 84–7, 91
Allsup, R., 61
Anderson, J., 86–7
anthropocentrism, 48
apprenticeship model, 9–10
apps, 46–7
Aristotle, 38
Artism Ensemble, 80
artist metaphor, 11–12, **12**
Arts Council England (ACE), 89–90
aspect perception, 41–2
Aston, Peter, 15, 16–17, 20–1, 49–50, 76
attentive listening, 43
autism spectrum, 46, 80
avant-garde musicians, 15

Baganda people, Uganda, 70–1
Bakan, M., 80
Baker, D., 7
Beardsley, M., 39
belonging, culture of, 32–4, 97–100
Bentley, Arnold, 17, 29
Bernhard, Christoph, 95
Bernstein, B., 78
Biesta, Gert, 96, 98–100, 103
Blacking, John, 29–30, 32, 64, 65, 73, 75, 97
Bourdieu, Pierre, 70, 71, 73
boutique metaphor, 11, **11**
Bowman, W., 101
Brazil, 98
bricolage, 40
British Music Information Centre, 88
Britten, Benjamin, 57–8
Bronfenbrenner, Urie, 74, 97
Bruner, Jerome, 42–3, 45
Budd, Malcolm, 26
Burton, Suzanne, 46–7

Cage, John, 27, 102
Campbell, P., 74, 79
Carnival of the Animals (Saint-Saëns), 41, 54–5, 57, 61
Chevé, Émile-Joseph-Maurice, 62
child-initiated musical interactions, 74–80
'children's music', adult conceptions of, 14–19, 70–4
Clark, T., 39
classical music, western, 7
  changing perspectives of, 29–30
  children's relationships with, 79–80

coiffuring musical childhood within, 71–2
custom and practice of listening to, 27–8, 43–4
experimental music as challenge to, 50–1
music as a language of emotions, 25, 27, 30
music delineating a story or narrative for children, 41, 54–61
privileging of, 29–30, 43–4, 96
cognitive development theory, 45, 76
Colwell, Richard, 29
competence, emphasis on, 28–30, 72–3, 94–7, 100–1
composition
  child-initiated, 75–6
  group, 45
  in music education, 44–5, 94–5
compositional attitude, 24
compound imagination, 39
Confucian ethics, 72
conscientisation, 34, 98
constructivist perspective on learning, 98–9
Contemporary Music Network, 88
Cook, Nicholas, 39
Cooke, Deryck, 25
Copland, Aaron, 39
Cox, Gordon, 15–16
creative listening, 42
creative music movement, 16–17
critical pedagogy, 33–4, 98, 103
cultural socialisation, 70–1
culture of belonging, 32–4, 97–100
culture of testing, 28–30, 94–7
curriculum, selection of musical content in, 14–19, 29, 54
Curwen, John, 62
cycle metaphor, 101
Cyprus, 79–80

Dairianathan, E., 71–2
d'Arezzo, Guido, 62
Davies, Stephen, 26–7
decolonisation, 103
Dennis, B., 15
Descartes, René, 38
designative meaning, 26
digital play, 46–7
Dunn, R., 42
Dutiro, Chartwell, 21, 81
Dzani, M., 76

early childhood care and education, 19
early childhood music education
  digital play in, 46–7
  Loud and Clear programme, 84–7, 91, 103